CHRIS AGOS

ACTING IN CHICAGO

*Making A Living Doing Commercials,
Voice Overs, TV/Film And More*

ISBN: 978-0-9828863-0-4
Visit www.actinginchicago.com for LCCN information.

For more information contact:

Tragos Ventures, Inc.
Evanston, IL 60202
www.tragosventures.com

Contents:

FOREWORD

The greatest thing in life to is be able to do what you love and get paid for it. That, to me, is success.

I have been in the business of show for the last 30 years doing what I love. At the age of 13 I worked professionally as an actor in Chicago, and by the age of 30 I was working on Broadway in New York City. The last decade of my life has been spent as a talent agent representing the finest actors in Chicago on projects ranging from feature films and television to commercials and shows on Broadway. These actors have won Emmys, Tonys and Oliviers.

The one thing that I have learned being on both sides of the business is this: just be yourself. You don't need to try to fit into a certain type. What makes you different, what makes you marketable, is the fact that you are comfortably you. Sounds pretty simple because it is. Being you is enough!

As an agent, what do I look for in an actor? I do not look for the actor that can morph into a serpent and then, in the next moment, pop into a cockney accent with an incredibly realistic limp. I look for the person who is genuine. A person who I can relate to. A person who has more interests in their life than just show business. I want to be able to see beyond your resume. I like to know your hobbies and find out what you're reading. I like to know that you are well rounded. I like a real person. After all, actors play people...not actors. Of course I look for skill and craft but the soul is what others connect to, not your resume.

Your job is to be yourself and control what you can control. Life is filled with many things that you can't anticipate. There's always the "ya never know" factor. Examples of things you can control are practical tasks like being prepared. If you receive a script and sides for an audition, read the script and memorize the sides. Always have pictures and resumes with you. Have your monologues ready to go at any point. Show up a little early to an audition. When an agent or casting director calls you for an audition, get right back to them. The list can go on and on. All of these things seem like common sense, but I continue to see them overlooked on a daily basis by the younger professionals that I represent.

The book that you are about to read is a dream for a guy like me that does what I do for a living. I spend a ton of time explaining "the business of the business" to actors who are unclear about how things work. I have read many books on how to have a career in show business. This book covers the things that you can control in the industry, and more importantly, the information is specific to Chicago. In a word: BAM! All I have to do now when we bring on a new actor is to have them read this book, and I've just gained back a 1/3 of my workday!

New York, Chicago and Los Angeles each have their own unwritten rules of protocol. You are about to get the inside scoop on the Chicago entertainment scene from the perspective of a very well-established working actor. As an agent in Chicago, I'd have to say that the information forthcoming is dead on. Put it to good use.

I wish you all the success that you deserve.

Sam Samuelson, Agent
Stewart Talent Management
Chicago - New York - Atlanta

CHAPTER ONE

What This Book Is, And Isn't

Fifteen years ago, a nervous, jittery college kid picked up the phone to call a teacher in Chicago. The kid prayed for an answering machine, because if the guy picked up, the kid didn't know what he would say. Thankfully, the machine *did* pick up. The kid listened to the outgoing message, then left a bumbling one of his own. A week later, he got a brochure in the mail. He looked it over, got scared again, and buried it in a desk drawer.

Fast forward one year. The kid found the brochure and looked it over. Without thinking, he called the teacher, who answered the phone this time. A conversation ensued. An appointment was made. A lesson was taken, and a career was launched.

That kid was me.

Today, I'm a working actor in Chicago. I don't have another job, I just act for a living. And I'm busy. The fact that I'm a full-time actor in the Midwest is unique enough. But what's different about my story is that I'm one of the few actors in town who is a product of the Chicago market itself. By that I mean, I didn't go to college to be an actor, and I had zero experience when I started. Everything I know I learned in Chicago's acting schools or on the job. No one in my family is an actor; and some folks would say that I have no formal training, which I guess I'd agree with. I started out knowing nothing and knowing no one in the business. The path from clueless college kid to career actor wasn't easy, and there were a lot of bumps along the way. But that's why I wrote this book - if you're looking to establish an acting career in Chicago, I know exactly what's on your mind. Because it was on mine, too.

If you're totally new to the industry, you might be thinking these things: How do I get started? Will I be "discovered"? Do I need an agent? How do I get one? Are there classes I can take? Where will I work? How much will I get paid? Do I work for myself or for a company? Is there some kind of application to fill out? When I was new, I pretty much just wanted to know how to get in.

If you're a veteran actor new to Chicago, you might need to know what kind of work is available for you here, or want details about which talent agents in town are strongest in your area of expertise. Maybe you're considering staying in Chicago for a while, then moving to a larger market. If you're going that route, you'll definitely want to learn what you can do to make the most of your time here.

When I decided I wanted to act for a living, I was a senior at DePaul University. I was a science major, and I had every intention of going to medical school. That meant lots of long nights studying for the Medical College Admission Test, the standardized exam all med school applicants take, and it's a monster. It takes a whole day, and it sucks the life right out of you. It's the kind of test you prepare for months in advance. Some people, like me, even take prep classes to help them get a higher score. To break the monotony of studying, I wanted something else to think about. When I found the brochure in my desk, it was the perfect escape.

The brochure contained information on private voice over coaching. I got the teacher's name from an ad in the paper. When I met with him and started reading some scripts, I knew I stunk, but I was hooked anyway. As a kid, I remember wanting to record myself doing something, anything, either on video or on audio tape. I recently discovered a cassette of me singing along to disco records when I was little. I think my favorite is my rendition of a Bee Gees hit. After my first voice over lesson, I knew I had a lot of work ahead of me if I ever wanted to be a paid voice over guy, but I also knew that I really wanted to do it. It was what I had been training for since I was little without even knowing it.

I didn't start out intending to be in the crazy world of acting. I thought actors were all hyper-creative, perennially poor, and chronically desperate for attention - turns out that some of them are. And I thought people who hire actors were coarse, unforgiving, brutal control freaks whom actors needed but didn't like - also sometimes true. My thought was, as someone who worked in voice over I'd avoid all that. Not true. The acting thing followed as a logical progression of my career. I had acted in plays in high school, but I never thought of myself as an actor until I looked at my records at the end of one particularly busy year. I keep track of what jobs I do, for whom I do them, and how much I make from each one. The IRS makes you do this for tax reasons, but it's also good for seeing where you've been, which allows you to decide where you want to go. When I saw that half my income came from on camera work, and the other half came from voice over jobs, I had somewhat of an epiphany: "Holy cow, I'm an actor." I guess I was the last one to find out.

Since I started, I've been cast in every kind of work Chicago has to offer. I've worked on TV commercials, films, industrials, cast in radio and other voice over work, booked on TV shows, shot for commercial print, worked as a hand model, hired for live corporate events, cast in theater, shot for the web, and I even did a musical once, though I don't really sing. I obviously came out of the shell I was hiding in when I called that voice over instructor. Now I spend my days going to and from auditions, shooting, recording, and generally winging my way through job after job. When I'm not auditioning or working, I have free time. I spend time with my family, I run, and I grocery shop during the day – when there's no wait at the checkout line. Sometimes I teach, sometimes I take a class. The best part is that I make a full-time living for working part-time hours. And if you think I have the life you want, wait until you read about a friend of mine later in the book.

If you ask around, you'll find that a lot of people like the way I work because I'm quick and I don't mess around on the set. When I'm working, I'm there for one purpose only: to get the job done. I feel the same way about this book. I'm going to give you all the information I wished I had when I started, so that you'll have as much insight as possible into Chicago's acting community. I'm going to present that information as efficiently as I can, because there's a lot to know. And most importantly, I'll make sure that you'll have everything you need to know if you want to make a living as an actor in Chicago. You'll just have to bring your abilities.

I should clarify a few things before we start. First, what do I mean by "making a living"? It's different for everyone. Some actors can barely pay their rent, or they have to skip the cable bill to pay their phone bill, and they're happy with that. If they can cover their monthly expenses, they would describe themselves as making a living. These are people who love what they do and are very dedicated to their art, but to whom money does not come easily for various reasons. If this describes your situation, look at this book as a guide to help you do much more of what you love to do.

I think most people strive to have more than what they need to just cover the basics. To me, making a living means you can make choices about what to do with your money, instead of your money making the choice for you. You're able to pay your bills, have money left over to save, and still be able to have a life. By this definition, you can do the things you want to do without putting your household at risk of financial meltdown. Things like taking vacations, having good credit, pursuing a pricey hobby, giving generously to a charity, or sending your kids to a private school won't be a burden to you. Basically, I'm talking about living a life of abundance, whatever that means to you.

Secondly, you should know that this book is not a how-to book on the art of acting. There are classes you can take and talented teachers out there whose job it is to help you learn how to act. Besides, you can't really learn this kind of thing from a book. You can get an idea of it, but you can't become a competent actor unless you're doing it in front of, and getting feedback from, a knowledgeable teacher. So if you're looking for something that will turn you into a brilliant thespian, this isn't it. If you're looking for all the information you'll need to build a career as an actor in Chicago, you've come to the right place. I'm assuming you can act. I'm assuming you've got a basic knowledge of what actors do, and that you want to make acting a profitable venture.

Finally, this book is written from my perspective, which is based on my experience over many years of working. We all draw conclusions based on the path we take. Because every actor's journey is different, these conclusions will vary from actor to actor. I suggest you read this book with an open mind. If something strikes you as contradictory to what you've heard or been told, it doesn't necessarily mean that either view is wrong. It just means that the two perspectives don't align.

It would be impossible for me to speak to everyone's specific set of circumstances or answer every question any reader might have, but I can promise these things: I promise to spill my guts about everything the business in this town has to offer. I'll even name names. I promise that everything you'll read is true, current and valid. I promise that this book will contain everything you'll need to start or cultivate an acting career in Chicago, and I'll leave nothing out. I promise to be straight with you, even if it's difficult to hear. Acting for a living can be a challenge, and if I didn't tell you about the difficult part of it, would you trust me to tell the truth about the other parts? Making all of this information work is up to one person: you. But you can do it. I know because I still do it every day, and many of my friends do, too.

Let's get busy.

CHAPTER TWO

First Thing's First

An actor friend of mine once shared a story with me. The day he told his dad he had decided to become an actor, his dad replied with one word. With his brow wrinkled and a scowl of confusion on his face, his father cleared his throat and asked, "Why?"

That's a fair question. For most of us actor types, we do it because we love it. There's something irresistible about being in front of people, pretending to be something you're not. The pull of the stage, or the camera, or the eyes of a crowd can be strong, allowing us to tap into instincts we can only count on when we're being watched, when an audience is depending on us for something. For some of us, performing recharges our batteries. But even though we might love acting, not everyone decides to make it a career. Pressures from family, society, or simple practicality prevail, and we choose much more sensible ways of making a living, ways that guarantee a regular paycheck but at the cost of cramming our creativity into a desk drawer. Acting can be a road to fame, wealth, and an exotic lifestyle, but it can also be the way to obscurity, sketchy finances, and vacationing only in your dreams. If you're in it for the superficial things, it's nothing but a roll of the dice. But if you simply can't imagine doing anything else, then it's a calling - and you can't say "no" when it calls.

Ask yourself this question: "Why do I want to act in Chicago?" Usually when I pose that question, people give me one of three reasons: they want to start here and then move on to a bigger market, they want a career that allows them to be creative, or they want to be stars. All are honest answers, but whenever I hear that someone got into acting to be a star, I have to wonder why they're in Chicago at all.

Chicago vs. Fame

When you decide to make the Midwest your home as an actor, you're making a choice between two very different but alluring things: work and fame. Here, you can be a newcomer or even moderately experienced, and there's work for you. There's a friendly, nurturing community that wants you to do well. There are people that will help you without expecting anything in return. As you progress up the ladder of work that's available, there's a greater chance of becoming a big fish in a small talent pool, allowing you to make a handsome living doing what you love.

But let's think about what isn't here. When you think of cities where movies and TV shows are made, you're probably more likely to think of Los Angeles or New York, and for good reason. New York hosts dozens of shows and films every year. Los Angeles produces hundreds. As of October 2010 there is one scripted TV show being produced in Chicago, Fox's *Ride-Along*. In the past we've had *The Beast* on A&E, and *Prison Break* on Fox, but they've either been canceled or left town. Detroit hosts one series, ABC's cop drama *Detroit 1-8-7*. Occasionally the show brings in Chicago actors for functionary roles. A few films are made here every year. They come in from L.A., shoot for a few weeks and then leave. They hire local actors for smaller parts, but most of the larger roles are played by actors hired in other markets, who are flown to Chicago to shoot. Actors become famous by doing TV and film. See where this is going?

When you're a Chicago actor, it's likely that your entire career will develop here. You can easily play out your dreams in any number of Chicago-based productions. However, if you stay in Chicago, you should brace yourself for the fact that working here will almost certainly not make you famous. Not one of the big time Chicagoans you can think of made it big by working here. The Cusacks, Jeremy Piven, Stephen Colbert, Chris O'Donnell, Alan Arkin, Vince Vaughn, and all the famous Second City and Steppenwolf actors had to move to Los Angeles or New York to become big shots. They may have gotten their start in the Midwest, but they earned their fame on one of the coasts.

But don't worry. Those who are in the know understand that Chicago is a great market to get started in. An actor can learn most everything they need to know about acting for a crowd or a camera in this city, and when they're ready, they can take that knowledge to L.A. or New York. Lots of recent college grads come here with that very intention. They come to build their resumes by working with the huge number of non-equity theater companies, grab some commercial work and maybe join the unions. After a couple of years they leave to go after bigger and hopefully better work. If you're in this group, moving here will be very rewarding, and will undoubtedly be an important step in your professional life.

If you're a Chicago-area native and you don't see yourself leaving, consider yourself lucky because you just happen to live in the third biggest market in the country. Actually, some would call Chicago the largest theater town in the United States. New Yorkers would argue that point, but there's no denying that with over 150 theater companies in town, there's an awful lot of acting going on here. Chicago is also home to some of the busiest advertising agencies in the nation and has a huge corporate video production presence. And we sometimes get to audition and work in smaller markets like Milwaukee and St. Louis. The bottom line is if you want to work here, there's no reason why you can't. Your toughest decision might be trying to figure out where to focus your energy.

Commercial vs. Theater Actors

In general, there are two types of actors in Chicago, the commercial actor and the theater actor. The basics of the two are the same; both are expected to give a truthful and believable performance. Generally, commercial actors work in front of cameras and microphones, and their performance is recorded to be played back on video, film, or audio tape at a later date. Theater actors work in front of live audiences and their performances are not recorded. What you see is what you get, and the next time it'll be a little (or maybe a lot) different than what you saw the last time. Different unions watch over each type of actor. The commercial actor may join one or both of the broadcast unions, either the American Federation of Radio and Television Artists (AFTRA) or the Screen Actor's Guild (SAG). The stage actor might join Actor's Equity Association (AEA). It's possible to join all three, of course, but each union has its own specific set of rules regarding when you can join. I'll explain more about unions later.

The lifestyle of the two kinds of actors can vary tremendously. Commercial actors work and audition during regular business hours: Monday through Friday, from 9:00 to 5:00. Occasionally they run across a job that shoots overnight, but for the most part acting is, in fact, a day job. In contrast, theater actors work mostly after dark. The larger theater companies rehearse their actors during the daytime, but performances are almost always in the evenings and on weekend afternoons (the one exception to this is children's theater, which is usually performed during the day). This contrast means that it's much easier for the theater actor to have a regular "day" job. If you work in commercials and you want to supplement your income, you'll need to have a job that allows you the flexibility to audition and work during the day, or you'll have to take a night job. And if you decide to act commercially and in theater at the same time, you'll have very little time available to make backup income.

The biggest lifestyle difference between the theater and commercial actor is earning potential. I know I'm going to break a lot of hearts by saying this, but you can't make a living doing theater in Chicago. Like any rule, this one has a few exceptions. There's a small group of Chicago-based actors who work at a very high level and are able to book show after show in theaters locally and around the country. These actors can do well financially, but for actors who aren't in this group, the earning potential is much greater in commercial work.

Another exception to this rule is the actor who works in musical theater. There are a handful of local companies that produce only Broadway-style musicals. I'm not talking about the big theaters downtown like the Cadillac Palace or the Auditorium Theater. Those houses bring in shows mostly from somewhere else, and almost the entire cast is imported, too. I'm talking about the smaller, but still very reputable theaters in the city and suburbs like Marriott's Lincolnshire theater and Drury Lane Oak Brook. In order to work in musicals, though, it helps to be a strong singer and dancer, as well as a strong actor. Performers who are good in all three disciplines are rare, so they tend to work a lot. And in Chicago, there is always a musical being produced somewhere. So if you're the musical type and you're good, you could go from job to job, and you'll have more earning power than your colleagues who only do straight theater.

Actors who have joined AEA, like the group of Chicago-based actors who get cast around the country, can earn good wages. The union makes sure they're taken care of because it sets the rates actors must be paid. But there's a real lack of theater companies in Chicago that hire Equity actors. The two most recognizable names, The Goodman and Steppenwolf, each have their own casting quirks. While the Goodman casts Chicago actors, they also like to cast from other markets, like New York. Steppenwolf has a large and diverse collection of company members to choose from. Translation: if you're not a company member, you're less likely to be in one of their shows. While a handful of other Equity companies exist, there simply isn't enough work for all of the Equity actors in Chicago to keep doing show after show. So, many supplement their theater income by doing commercial work.

The overwhelming majority of live theater in Chicago is happening in storefront spaces and being done by actors who aren't affiliated with AEA. Audiences will see innovative, powerful performances in these theaters, but they simply can't afford to pay their actors a living wage. It's a simple fact of economics. They can only charge so much for a ticket. After paying all the costs to produce the show, most often there's very little left over for the actors. Most theater companies go after donations and grants, but usually this money only goes so far.

The commercial folks win the money game hands down. But if you think I'm discouraging you from doing theater, nothing could be further from the truth! I'm simply making a distinction between the earning power you'll have in both worlds. Theater is an important part of a Chicago actor's time here. Being on stage gives you lots of credibility with the decision makers in town, and not doing any theater at all can actually get in the way of your effort to make a living. It's important to go after a certain number of theater roles, because they can be an integral part of your career path. But when it comes to money, there's no getting around this fact: there's a ton of dough to be made in the commercial acting community, you just have to decide to go and get your share. Later, we'll talk about how much your share can be.

What's A Workday Like?

Free time can be your best friend or your worst enemy, but however you think it'll affect you, get ready to have a lot of it. The full-time Chicago actor's day can be filled with auditions and jobs, or it can be filled with nothing more pressing than walking down to the mailbox to see if there's a check waiting for you. Let's take a look at a day with a little bit of everything going on.

A career actress, we'll call her Faith, starts her day with an audition at a casting director's office for a regional TV commercial. It's for an automaker, and they're looking to cast a few friendly looking people to be featured shopping for, and buying, one of their cars. Her audition time is 10:00 a.m., but the casting director is running a little late, so by the time the audition is over and she's walking out of the office, it's almost 11:00. That's ok, because she still has plenty of time to get to her next audition, which isn't until 1:00. With two hours to kill, she decides to visit one of her agents to pick up a check for a job she recently did. A little chatting, a couple of questions about work that's going on around town, and she's just about overstayed her welcome. No problem, it's time for lunch anyway. A quick sandwich will get her through her second audition of the day, a voice over audition for a radio spot. It's at a different agent's office. A fast food chain is looking for just the right voice to promote their new breakfast item. Faith goes in, does her thing, then leaves. She's done for the day except for a scene study class that evening. Until then, she's got free time. She heads to her class (which goes swimmingly), and then she's home for the night.

That's a pretty solid day with good things going on. Faith didn't make any money, but she laid the groundwork for a couple of potentially big jobs, and she can't get the work without auditioning. You'll have many just like this, but you'll also experience the strain of having nothing to do at all, as well as the elation of having so much to do in a day that it doesn't seem like it will all get done. I sometimes have days where I literally have so much going on that I have to turn some of it down. I also have gone entire weeks with only one audition. That's part of the business, sometimes you're up, and sometimes you're not. But before you get into the business at all, you've got to get your ducks lined up in a nice, neat little row.

CHAPTER THREE

The Seven Ways (Besides Theater) Actors Make Money in Chicago

Now that I've totally burst your bubble and implied that if you do theater you're going to be digging through your couch cushions for spare change, let's talk about what *can* make you a living in this market. I don't want to keep you from doing theater, but if you're striving to earn your primary income from acting, you're much more likely to reach that goal by working commercially.

The rest of this book is going to focus on the side of acting that pays well. As fun and invigorating as theater is, for most actors it's generally not a practical way of earning money in Chicago. And that's what you want to do, right? You want to be an actor, *and* be able to pay your bills. Here's how.

There are seven ways that actors in Chicago make a living:

- Commercials
- Industrials
- Voice Over
- Print
- Trade Shows/Live Events
- Ear Prompter
- TV/Film

I'll explain each one. You know what some of them are, but the meaning of others may not be as obvious.

Commercials

Commercials (also called spots) are exactly what you think. We're talking about the :30 or :60 second commercials that come on during your favorite TV shows. They also show up online. They can be annoying, intrusive and loud, but they make money for the actors that are in them. And for some of us, commercials make up the majority of our work.

I think it's important to understand how a spot gets made so you can understand where the actor fits in. Here's a simplified description of the process: A commercial starts with a product or service that needs some publicity. Let's say it's a new car. The car is made by a company, which hires an advertising agency to market the car. The ad agency people talk with the car company people about how they think the car should be promoted, what kind of image it should have, who might be the target buyer, and other things that will shape what the advertising will look like. Then the ad agency people go back to their office and come up with a few ideas for the car company to look at. When a concept is agreed upon, commercial scripts are written and submitted for approval. Let's say one of those gets green lit for production. The ad agency then hires a production company, which is a firm that specializes in the production of commercials, hence the name. The production company works with the ad agency to make sure that the spot comes out exactly as it was pitched to and approved by the car company. So they hire the crew (a director, set designers, wardrobe stylists, etc.) and they hire the actors. The production company holds an audition, often run by a casting director. A casting director's job is to sort through all the talent (meaning actors) that might be right for the spot, bring them in to audition, and present the results to the production company and the ad agency, who will ultimately decide which actors to use. Once the actors are chosen, the spot gets made, aired, and then retired when it's no longer needed.

We'll talk more about casting directors and auditions later. But I wanted you to have an idea of how complex the process is before you (the actor) ever get involved. Commercials are open to all ages and types of actors: young, old, beefy, skinny, quirky, studly, intellectual, goofy, and everything in between. After working in this business a little, you'll find that you fit into a "type" like "college kid," or "young mom." Your type will depend a lot on how old you look and how you present yourself, but there's work for every type out there, from creepy to wholesome.

Industrials

The word "industrial" is sort of a loose term, but generally refers to productions that don't get broadcast to the general public on TV. They're targeted to a much more specific, and therefore limited, audience. Let's say there's a company that wants to get some product information into the hands of American farmers. They can do it effectively by producing a video that's just shown to farmers, either by posting it on a specialized website or by mailing the farmers a DVD. This allows the company to bypass the expense and time constraints of a TV spot, and target their audience much more efficiently. These videos are basically long commercials, maybe five or ten minutes instead of thirty seconds, and very often, they need actors. Sometimes actors are hired to play out a scene (like two farmers talking about the product) and sometimes an actor is hired to portray a member of the company, like a spokesperson. If the actor talks directly to the audience by looking into the camera, that's called on camera narration.

Another example of an industrial is a training video. Let's say an insurance company needs to teach new agents how to sell their policies. There are lots of ways to show people how to sell insurance, and one of those ways is to watch it being done. A video may be produced with a bunch of scenes between an insurance agent and a customer. Scripts are carefully written to make sure that the agent in the video is following all of the company's sales policies and procedures, and the customer is responding realistically. Then, actors are hired to play out the scenes. Why don't they just use their own sales people in these videos? Sometimes they do, but salespeople are in sales, they're not actors. So even though they're talking about something they're very familiar with, they still can't read a script like an actor can. We've trained for that, they haven't. So usually companies hire professional actors to get professional results.

Companies typically hire actors that look like their employees. Not literally, of course, but if you look more at home sitting on a Harley than pushing papers in a bank, you're going to get called in for jobs that need a tougher look. Conversely, if you look like Joe Stock Broker, you won't be considered for the tough-guy stuff, but for the more business-oriented shoots.

Companies also look for actors who are age-appropriate for the roles they're being hired for. If a scene is between two mid-level managers, you're not going to get that audition if you're 23, because mid-level managers are usually older. Also, if a company's workforce is made up mostly of people in their 30's and 40's, you'll probably need to be in that age range to be considered for their job. I've missed out on plenty of jobs because I was too young or too old. Most industrial work will go to people between the ages of 25 and 50, but that doesn't mean there aren't opportunities for those outside of this age range.

Chicago is a BIG market for this kind of work. This is the one thing we do more of here than any other market in the country. It's our bread and butter, and you can build a whole career just around industrial work. Many industrials require actors to use the ear prompter, a handy thing I'll explain in a bit.

Voice Over

When you listen to a radio commercial, or watch a TV spot and a voice is heard but not seen, you're listening to a voice over (VO). You know the guys who do the movie trailers? Voice overs. People who do voice over work are called either voice overs or voice talent. Either way you say it, you could be rolling in dough if you decide to stay off camera.

Voice talent work in all kinds of media: TV, radio, film, commercials, industrials, web, video games, toys, books on tape, children's books, and elevators (you know, the guy that says "25th floor" when you get out on the 25th floor?) I'm even the voice of a treadmill – no, I'm not kidding. There's a company that makes a machine which offers a virtual personal trainer feature to help motivate you through your workouts. You can pick between a male or female trainer, and I was hired as the voice of the guy.

When I'm teaching VO, one of the first questions people ask me is, "Do you think I have a good voice?" And my reply is always, "It doesn't matter, there's work for everyone." That's true, but it's also true that there's more work available for some people than others. Being a good voice talent involves so much more than just the quality of your voice. It's really about the read, or how you say the words of the script, rather than how clear, deep, or resonant your voice sounds. If I say the word "announcer", what kind of image comes to mind? Most people picture an older gentleman with a big, deep voice talking into a microphone with one hand up to his ear, but those days and those announcers are long gone. Sure, there are plenty of deep-voiced VO guys out there, but most talent today have everyday sounding voices. If you talked to them on the phone you probably wouldn't think they did VO. But whatever they have, they know how to turn it on in front of a mic, and that's why they work. Most of the best voice talent come from an acting background because it's about how well you read the script, versus how great your voice sounds. So it's logical for an actor to also do voice over work. As long as you're good at bringing life to scripts, there's work for you whether you have a high-pitched whiny voice or an everyday run-of-the-mill voice.

The second thing I'm often asked is, "Do you think I could get into it?" And my answer is always a resounding "Maybe." VO isn't for everyone, but it's for more people than you might think. I have strong feelings on the subject. I think that if you're trying to make a living as an actor in Chicago, you simply have to explore it. If you don't, you're limiting yourself. In fact, I think you're making the choice to not do as much as you can in order to have a successful career. My career is split nearly even between VO and on camera work, so it's been essential to my ability to make a living. But working in voice over isn't easy. It's competitive, and it's expensive to get started. There are classes to take, and voice demos to make. A demo is a minute's worth of audio that showcases what you can do. When you're new, demos have to be created from scratch instead of using work that you've already done; and they have to be produced by people who know what they're doing. Those people cost money, but the investment can be worth it. Check out how much voice talent make in chapter 10.

A word of caution: there are some folks whose chances for VO work will be extremely limited. If you speak English with a heavy foreign accent, you'll be eliminated from nearly every job except those that require your accent. The same thing applies if English is your first language, but you have a strong regional accent. If you're from New York and everyone can tell when you open your mouth, there's less work for you than if you lost the accent. If you've got a speech impediment such as a lisp or a stutter, you should work with a therapist to make as much of that go away as possible before pursuing this kind of work. Folks with those challenges just don't get hired. If a job requires someone with a stutter, a producer will just hire a talent they know and tell them to do the stutter rather than look for someone with an actual stutter.

The bottom line is VO can be a lucrative addition to your tool belt as a Chicago actor, but it takes specific training to be able to do it well. Just because you can read out loud doesn't mean you're a good voice talent. So if you're interested in this kind of work, get yourself into a class. That's the only way you'll discover if VO could be for you. I'll explain more about training later in the book.

Trade Shows/Live Events

Trade shows are ultra-organized conventions where companies from a specific industry, like restaurant equipment makers or microchip manufacturers, gather to show their wares. Corporations rent booth space on the floor of convention centers, and spend huge amounts of money decorating and styling them to best reflect their agenda at the show.

A trade show offers several different opportunities for working actors. You can be a host, which often just involves handing out promotional items. You can be a crowd gatherer, which involves chatting with people and encouraging them to visit the booth. You could be a product specialist, who is someone that has been trained by the client to speak about their product or service one-on-one with show attendees. You could also be hired as a presenter. These are the guys and girls who deliver presentations in the booth in front of live audiences of show attendees. These presentations may or may not include additional elements such as multimedia shows, product demonstrations, even rock bands or comedians. In other words, actors are hired to do anything to attract people's attention and keep them in the booth.

Hosts, crowd gatherers and product specialists come from all walks of life. Clients don't just hire actors, they may hire graphic designers, print models, students, fashion designers, salespeople, or whomever can easily strike up a conversation with a stranger. All three are expected to interact with the public, so people skills are a must.

If you are, or look and behave like you're at least 30 years old and are a good public speaker, then you could be a candidate to be a presenter. Presentation work is also sometimes called narration. Just like with industrials, companies like to hire actors that fit with the company's image. If you're more the grubby mechanic type, you'd be a candidate to present at the construction equipment shows. If you're a young hipster, you'll be doing the technology shows. If you're an attractive woman you should be able to work just about any show.

Trade show work has pluses and minuses for actors. On the one hand, it's relatively long-term work, which is great. An industrial or commercial shoot might be one or two days long, but a trade show could run four or five days. Plus, there's usually a rehearsal day before the show opens, and there might be one day on either end of the job for travel if the show isn't in your home city. So if you're in Chicago and you travel to work the Consumer Electronics Show in Las Vegas, you're gone a full week because it's a five day show. In terms of a paycheck, this is great because trade shows are high paying jobs, and you're getting paid for every day that you're gone. This is much better than sitting at home doing nothing, right? In addition, sometimes a company will hire you to do multiple shows, meaning that you can count on having work throughout the year. The downside is that you're not included on any auditions back home when you're gone. You might miss something really great, but you can't complain because you're working, and that's the best reason to miss out on a job.

It starts to get a little tricky if you do a lot of trade shows, which means you're gone a week or two every month. If doing trade show work is something you want to do and you're happy with it, you're in heaven. Financially, you'll be doing very well. But if trade shows ultimately aren't where you want to be, then you're giving up something for that financial gain. You have to wonder what you're missing out on when you're gone so much. For one, you can forget about doing theater if you're frequently out of town because you'll miss too many rehearsals. Secondly, is your agent not submitting you for as many jobs because you're usually not available? You can't make your agent money when you're out of the loop. Perhaps most importantly, are you missing out on the few TV and film auditions that come along? If you're interested in working here in order to build your resume, and then move on to L.A., no one there is going to care that you work a trade show every other week. They're going to want to see what TV and film work you've done. So even though the trade show money will be rolling in, you'll be sidetracked from your ultimate goal. Just something to think about.

Print

The term "print" covers any job where an actor's photograph is taken with a still camera. The photo might be used anywhere, such as in magazine and newspaper ads, online banner ads, trade publications, product packaging, mailers, point-of-purchase displays, billboards or catalogs. You might think that models, not actors, are used for this kind of stuff, and a lot of times they are. But there are jobs that call for "real people", a term ad agencies use to describe folks who aren't fashion models. These are people who look like everyone else, and could be the girl who rings up your groceries or the guy who delivers your mail.

For obvious reasons, this work is all about how you look. If you have the look the client is hunting for, you'll be in the running for the job. The acting thing is secondary, though it still counts because all print jobs are going after some kind of "feel" the model must emote. You might need to be really excited, confident or confused, and you've got to be able to connect with that state of mind and actually look like you're excited, confident or confused.

A number of years ago, a friend of mine got a print job, and the shoot was on location in a bowling alley. These days, when you go on a print audition (also called a look-see) your test shots are taken digitally and posted online for the client to review. Back then, they snapped Polaroids of you and delivered them to the client in a box. When my friend showed up at the job, she happened to walk by the table the agency was using to organize the paperwork for the job, and she spotted her Polaroid. On it, in small handwriting, was "Looks like a bowler." That's why she got the job. She didn't know what that meant, the fact that someone thought she looked like a bowler, but she was happy to have the cash.

Sometimes print jobs come as a bonus with on camera jobs like commercials and industrials. I once did a series of TV spots for a medical association, and they also wanted to use my image in their print campaign. The print work was negotiated as a separate job with its own fee, because the TV shoot only entitled them to use my likeness for TV. So for that job I was paid twice: once for TV and once for print.

Print is great work if you can get it, because the jobs are usually quick and pay fairly well. The downside is that it takes longer to get paid for print work for a variety of reasons, one of which is that it's not covered by a union. More about unions later.

TV/Film

I've already talked about the relative lack of TV or film being shot in Chicago, but that's not to say that it's impossible to get this kind of work, it's just rare. As of this writing there is only one scripted TV show regularly shooting in Chicago. Typically the main actors (called series regulars) are cast in L.A. and brought to Chicago to shoot. The smaller roles are open to local actors, and we're glad to have them. This work usually goes to the more established actors in town. That's not to say that you won't be considered if you're new, but you better have a great audition. If you don't, the decision makers will assume you're not ready for this work, and you probably won't get a second chance for a while.

Chicago also has some unscripted TV projects which are being shot around town. A handful of shows that air on HGTV shoot here, but they've got their designer/hosts already and rarely replace them. Occasionally there's some reality TV shot here, but that's not for actors, it's for people who just want to be on TV. There are a handful of companies producing television from Chicago, but they either shoot or cast somewhere else.

Film work is difficult to get in Chicago because there's so little of it. I should make a distinction here: Hollywood-based film work is scarce, but there are plenty of student and independent films produced all the time. There's room for both if you want to do this kind of work, but there's a big difference between how you go about getting hired.

For the big budget studio films that shoot here like *The Dark Night*, *Road to Perdition*, and *Public Enemies*, nearly all of the main actors are cast in L.A. That means Chicagoans don't have a shot at those roles. We get the smaller parts, which sometimes can be really good ones. I have several friends who had multiple days or weeks shooting on these films. To be considered for this work, you have to go through whichever casting director is working on the film, which is usually Claire Simon Casting or Tenner/Paskal/Rudnicke Casting. O'Connor Casting does work on film, but they are very strong in commercial, industrial and even print and VO auditions.

Smaller budget independent films sometimes use casting directors, but other times they just call agents directly for auditions. Ultra low budget and student films, on the other hand, usually bypass the traditional casting avenues and advertise on Craigslist to find talent. These are a crapshoot in the sense that you never know what the experience will be like. Some of these projects are well organized and run very professionally, and some consist of two clueless guys with a borrowed video camera. My advice is to go after any and all opportunities if you're new to the business. However if you've been on a set before, be more selective about which projects you choose to work on. Ask lots of questions and get as much information as possible about what working conditions are going to be like, whether you're going to be paid, and what kind of time commitment the project requires before you even go to the audition. You'll save yourself a lot of hassle if you cover your bases first, and know what you're getting into before committing time to it.

Ear Prompter

If you don't know what an ear prompter is, you're going to thank me for introducing it to you. Ear prompters let you deliver your lines word for word, without memorizing them or holding a script in your hand. It's sometimes rightfully referred to as the actor's secret. (In the business, ear prompters are commonly referred to as "the EAR". I can't tell you why it's always capitalized, but whenever you see it on a resume or in a casting notice, it's always written in caps. So to avoid any confusion I'm going to use that notation going forward.)

EARs consist of an earpiece, either wired (like news anchors use) or wireless (like a hearing aid), connected to a small recorder. The system is being used correctly when all of the pieces are hidden from view. You record your script and play it back through your earpiece. As you hear the script, you recite it like you would a memorized piece. The trick is to make it look like the words are coming off the top of your head. This is a talent in and of itself, because it's not easy to talk while you're listening to a voice in your head and be convincing at the same time. After all, you still have to act. But if you can master this skill, you'll open up a whole new way of making money.

EARs are lifesavers. They remove the stress of not knowing your script, they allow writers to make changes on the set, and they take the pressure off of producers to get a script to you far in advance. This is the main reason why producers request actors who are ear prompter proficient.

Actors mostly use the EAR for industrials and trade shows, but there are other places it can be used. A friend of mine in L.A. used his EAR while shooting an episode of *The West Wing*. The writers rewrote his monologue minutes before he was to shoot it, so he went into his trailer, recorded it, and did it flawlessly on the first take. No one on the set knew how he memorized the new text so quickly. They also come in handy when you have a last-minute commercial audition. You can walk into the room looking like you've got the script memorized.

A few years ago, I was auditioning for a series of beer spots, and I laid the scripts down on my EAR before going into the room. I had a great audition and the clients surprised me by asking me to read a few more spots for them. They pulled three out of a folder and asked me to look at them and come back when I was ready. I walked out as the next actor entered. Then, while in the waiting room I recorded the new spots, went through them once or twice, and by the time they were ready for the next audition, I was ready to show them the new stuff. They were surprised I was ready so quickly. I went in, did the scripts perfectly, and they were stunned by my super-duper memory! I thanked them for all the compliments, and didn't tell them my secret. I also didn't get the job, but that's another story.

The EAR isn't for everyone. Some actors pick up the skill very quickly and have no trouble listening, talking, and being natural at the same time. Others struggle, and struggle hard. I'd say the average actor can take an eight-week class and be pretty competent on the EAR by the end of it. Some people will pick it up much faster, others take more time. The only way to find out where you fit in is to try it out. As far as cost goes, you can get current pricing on several websites. Search online for some examples, but generally you can count on spending $1000 to $2000 for a complete kit and a class. If that sounds like a lot, keep in mind that one or two jobs will pay for it.

I count the EAR as a separate way actors make a living because it's possible to work in all aspects of the business without ever knowing that it even exists. Plenty of actors do, but if you take the time to learn how to use the EAR, you'll be rewarded in ways you can't yet imagine.

Wrap Up

You can think of the things on this list as bricks in the actor's career wall. An industrial brick is laid next to a VO brick, which is rested on top of a TV brick and all three of these are supported by a commercial brick. Why? Because Chicago is the *third* largest market in the country, not *the* largest. There isn't enough of one kind of work here to let everyone focus only on the one thing they really like to do. Full-time actors here are much more likely to be working in multiple disciplines with the rare exception, of course. If you're a model you can do very well sticking with print, and there are also some people who just work in VO. But for the rest of us, we've got to work on building our wall.

A strong foundation of knowledge is the only way to make sure your wall is going to hold up. For that, you need training, and you're in luck, because Chicago is a great place to learn.

CHAPTER FOUR

Learning (or Perfecting) The Ropes

If you think acting looks easy, it's because you've been watching good actors who have trained hard. They've spent a lot of time practicing to make it look simple, and it's paid off. Acting is not easy, it's difficult, and it takes training to get your body and mind attuned to the ways in which you can create believable relationships and interactions on demand. If you're thinking that you'll be able to walk untrained into Chicago's acting community and compete with actors who have been working for years, you're going to be disappointed. Everyone has a certain amount of natural talent, but it takes some instruction to learn to put it to use. Besides that, you'll need some knowledge of the language used in the industry, and classes are a great way to learn in a stress-free environment. If you're coming to Chicago after working in another market, a class will allow you to get to know your way around the business here.

What classes you take and where you take them will depend on a number of factors: whether or not you come from an acting background, what kind of work you want to do, and what skills you'll need to work in your selected area. If you're just beginning and don't have any education under your belt, then you'll need to get yourself into a basic acting class. All of the schools I'll mention will offer this kind of class, and if you're new to acting, it's a must. An intro to acting class will teach you any number of very useful and helpful things that you'll use throughout your career. So if you haven't done so already, put acting 101 at the top of your list. It's the only way to start.

If you're not exactly a beginner, but you have no real professional experience as an actor, it may be helpful for you to take a more advanced acting class. These are aimed at students who have acted on stage a few times, and know some of the fundamental concepts and terminology on which actors rely. Typically the more advanced-level classes are oriented around scene study, where you and a partner are given a scene to work on and present in front of the class. For the actor whose experience has been limited to only high school or college stages, these classes can be an eye-opening experience because they allow the actor to work with all different types and ages of partners. Check with each school to see if you're a good fit for these courses. Some schools require an audition for admittance, or completion of a lower level class first. I'd say if you've been on stage a few times and have a fair amount of confidence in your ability, you'll probably get a lot out of these kinds of classes. Stick with the intro classes if you're a beginner, otherwise you may not be admitted to the class, and if by chance you are, you may not fit in well with the experienced actors for whom the class was designed.

For the actor who has done a good amount of stage work, has a concrete grasp of the ideas behind solid relationship development, and would like to start making some money instead of donating their time to the theater, it's time to diversify. Stay with me here, I'm not talking about diversification from an economic standpoint, but I am going to borrow the term from the world of finance.

If you've done any investing at all, you know about the principle of diversification. It simply means that you don't put all of your money in one place. Instead, you spread it around among a few different places. Say you've got ten thousand dollars burning a hole in your pocket. The number of places you can invest it is infinite. On some trusted advice you decide to diversify by putting a portion of it in the bank where's it's insured by the FDIC, a portion in a few stocks, and maybe the rest in a bond mutual fund. This way, if the stock market tanks or the bond market slides, then the entire ten thousand dollars doesn't go with it. You still have some of your money because it's spread out among different investment vehicles, and it's not all in the one that decreased in value. On the other hand, you'll still see some gains when either market goes up. By diversifying, your total investment is much more stable, and much less likely to suffer from fluctuations in any one area.

If you think of your acting career as your total investment, and the talent and skills you have to offer as the actual dollars, you can begin to see my point. If you spread those skills around multiple areas of opportunity, you're much less likely to be effected by a downturn in any one of them. You're much more likely to have a stable income across your career, and be able to take advantage when things are busy if you're going after work in every area that's right for you.

The acting business was pretty shaken up by the recession that began in late 2008. The effects of it might still be lingering as you read this. When companies tighten their belts, actors feel the crunch, and this recession hit our business hard. Many actors closed the door on their careers. The volume of auditions and work declined to the point where they just couldn't make much money.

Many of those folks were not diversified. They concentrated on commercials, or they were really heavy into voice over. I even heard of a model or two going back home because there wasn't much work for them. They had no control over the nation's economy whatsoever, but the downturn hit them harder since they put all their proverbial eggs in one basket.

On the other hand, if they were trained in all seven ways actors in Chicago make money, they might have been able to ride out the storm. They would have felt the sting a little, but they would have had other sources of income to pick up the slack. I sure felt the sting, but I was fortunate. My income only dropped about 7% from 2008 to 2009. The variety of work I do had everything to do with that. Had I focused on just one thing, I may have been in trouble too.

Unlike investing money where the list of places to put it is endless, when it comes to acting in Chicago, you've only got seven places to invest your time, skills and effort. Concentrating on only one of them is a good path to disappointment and financial headaches. There are rare exceptions, but most of the career actors in town are very versatile and work in every facet of this business. It's the best approach to putting together a long lasting, stable career. In an unpredictable business like ours, it's better to plan for unexpected changes than be caught off guard.

The simplest way to sum up how a stage actor or model can diversify is this: get yourself on camera and behind a microphone. When I say on camera, most people think that I'm talking about movies and TV. If you were reading about acting in NYC or L.A., that would be correct, but since we're talking about Chicago, I mean work in industrials and commercials. Almost all the acting schools in Chicago have specialized courses that focus on acting for the camera, which is very different than acting on a stage. Think of it this way: the stage is like a message on a billboard, and the camera is like a message on a greeting card. Advertisers who want to get your attention with a billboard will use big fat fonts and flashy colors because that's what it takes to make it easy for you to understand their message while you're zooming down the highway. In contrast, the message contained in a greeting card doesn't need to be as blatantly obvious. Subtlety plays much better here just like it does on camera. Billboards scream at you, greeting cards whisper. Stage acting is typically big and flashy;

acting for the camera requires a gentler approach. When I tell you to get yourself behind a microphone, I'm talking about voice over. I've already mentioned how important VO is to my career, and it could be important for you as well, but you won't know until you try it out in a class.

Since you've made the choice to be an actor, and you understand that your chances of making a living are much higher if you work in many different areas, you'll need training to be able to do that work. Below I've outlined the classes you should consider for each of the seven ways (besides theater) Chicago actors generate income, along with where to go for them. Before I do that, though, I want to make something clear. The schools I'm going to mention are reputable, well-known training centers that have been in operation for a long time. I've taken or taught classes at most of these places, and if I haven't, I personally know the people running the place. I do not get kickbacks for writing about these schools, and the only reason I'm willing to recommend them by name is because I trust them to do a good job training you at a fair price.

Commercials

I consistently recommend three schools to actors of all levels when they ask me where they should take a class for commercials: Act One Studios, Acting Studio Chicago, and The Green Room.

Act One Studios

Act One Studios bills itself as the Midwest's largest acting school, and they just might be right. They offer a large variety of classes and seminars from beginning acting through master's classes for working professionals. They've also gone a step further by offering a conservatory program, something that is unique in Chicago's acting schools. It's a full-time, two-year training program that's an alternative to a Master's Degree program from a university. If that's a little much for you, Act One Studios also offers three classes focused specifically on working in commercials. Years ago I took my very first class at Act One because I heard it had a good reputation in the business. That's still true today, and part of the reason why is that they maintain focus on solid acting techniques. According to their website, "The emphasis in our camera classes is on taking your acting skills and adjusting them to a specific medium. Keeping your acting alive while dealing with the physical and technical restrictions of the camera."

Act One is probably the supermarket of Chicago's acting schools. By that I mean that it's got the greatest variety of classes and has the largest facility with the highest amount of people going through their programs. I think most actors in town have studied there at one time or another. Their location is decent, though parking in the neighborhood can be challenging. If you're taking the CTA, they're in between the Red and Brown lines, and several bus routes run right in front of their building. Word around town is that the quality of the instruction is still high, so I'd check them out at www.actone.com

Acting Studio Chicago

Not to be outdone, Acting Studio Chicago is also an excellent place to study acting for the camera. The studio has been in existence in one form or another since 1981. It was started by actress Jane Brody, who had been working with Michael Shurtleff, a leading casting director and author of *Audition*, an influential book on the audition process (and a great read, I recommend you pick up a copy). Brody realized that his approach to acting was a valuable tool that wasn't being taught in Chicago, so she opened a studio called The Audition Centre to share the method with other actors. The early 1990's, however, brought a change of ownership and a new name. Rachel Patterson, the studio's owner and director for nearly twenty years, has grown it into a well-respected school with a great word-of-mouth following among Chicago's actors. They've accomplished that by striving to give each student a unique experience as they move through their training. Patterson says, "We really pride ourselves on giving personal attention to all our students. We try to be an artistic home for them, so even if they're not currently registered in a class, they're always welcome to come by and chat. We have an open door policy and have no problem giving out advice on resumes, or looking at headshots, or just talking about the steps the actor might be able to take to move ahead in their career." Being a former actor and casting director, Patterson has a lot of street cred in town. She and her staff are more than qualified to guide any actor through the maze of work available in Chicago. They're straightforward about the realities of the business, but still very supportive of what each actor wants to accomplish. Parking in their neighborhood is difficult at best, but they're a short walk from the CTA Red Line, and they also offer discounted parking for students at some nearby garages.

Acting Studio Chicago's on camera classes are a great place to start exploring the finer points of being a commercial actor and can serve as a one-stop shop to learn all about acting on camera. Their core camera program is divided into three levels, each building on the skills taught in the previous level. Additionally there are classes that focus solely on commercials and others with an emphasis on the business side of acting. Check out www.actingstudiochicago.com for details and current offers.

The Green Room

The Green Room is another stellar place to study commercial acting. Run by Sean Bradley and David Murphy, both actors and former casting directors, it was founded for the purpose of training actors in the art of working in commercials. The Green Room's curriculum was drawn from their experience of watching thousands of commercial auditions while working at O'Connor Casting, one of Chicago's busiest casting offices. At O'Connor they saw the good, the bad and the horrible, and decided that the city's actors needed to change the way they approach auditioning. While a lot of actors did a terrific job, Sean says, "There were some who were solid in a stage performance, but totally dropped the ball when it came to a commercial audition. They just weren't competitive on a national level. They were great actors, but their auditions made Chicago look bad on a national stage." Knowing that more producers would cast in Chicago if the talent pool was doing fantastic auditions time after time, The Green Room opened to show good actors how to make their on camera auditions great.

Sean points out that they don't use any particular method in their commercial classes. Instead, their instruction comes from real-world experience and instincts that they've developed from years of watching actors do fantastic auditions or crash and burn. Their core program is a five-level process designed for a student to complete within a year, the first three levels of which focus solely on commercial training.

I'd recommend The Green Room for actors who have some experience behind them; however, that's not to say that beginners aren't welcome there. "Having someone new in class is sometimes great because they don't come in with all the acting baggage that experienced actors do," says Sean. That baggage can be difficult to drop when searching for new ways to be real on camera. Visit www.thegreenroomstudio.tv for their current offerings.

Industrials/Ear Prompter

If you're interested in getting some specialized training in acting for industrials, Act One Studios has offered their EAR/Industrial class for well over fifteen years now. This is where I learned how to be a pro on the ear prompter. The nice thing about the class is that earpieces and recorders are provided. You can try the EAR out before you decide to buy your own system, which could save you a ton of money down the road. If you find it's not for you, you're only out the cost of the class, which is a whole lot better than buying an ear prompting system that you can't use or sell.

The course is nicely broken up into several phases, each teaching a skill with the intention of layering new skills over it in future phases. Students begin with a review of acting for the camera, then move into using the EAR, and it's not long before you're doing both at the same time, which is what you'll need to do on the job. Instructors use real scripts from past jobs, so the work students do in class is as realistic as possible. Want to know how to handle props while on an EAR? Or how to tackle techno babble? Or how to do a scene with two other actors while you're on the EAR but they aren't? You'll learn it here. By the end, you'll have a good grasp of the kinds of situations you're likely to deal with in the real world and be on your way to knowing how to handle them.

Acting Studio Chicago also offers a course on the EAR, developed and occasionally taught by yours truly. Students in this class have the additional benefit of learning how to use a TelePrompTer. Neither school schedules the class during every term, so check their respective websites for your next opportunity to sign up.

Voice Over

In my mind, Chicago really only has one place to go for VO training and that's Acting Studio Chicago. Offering three class levels plus a few specialized seminars, Acting Studio Chicago covers all the bases and has fantastic instructors. I know because I used to be one of them, and still fill in now and then.

If you're new, start with Beginning VO with Dave Leffel. Dave brings an interesting combination of knowledge to the class because he's not only a voice talent; he's also a sound engineer. He works on the other side of the glass every day recording and editing spots for clients. He knows how to get a good performance from a student, and he will pass along real world examples of what producers say they need from their voice talent. You'll spend a few weeks learning in a classroom and the last few in a professional recording studio so you can see what it's like to work with the real deal. By the end, you'll know what the VO business is like so that you can decide whether or not to pursue it more. The class is a fantastic value considering what you get, and I can't recommend it highly enough.

Once you're ready to step up to a more advanced level of training, head to Jeff Lupetin's Intermediate VO class. Jeff is a longtime industry pro, with tons of big name VO credits. He also really enjoys teaching and is great at coaxing out terrific performances from talent because he's also a freelance director. In his class you'll study the finer points of voicing spots, animation and narration in a professional studio. Jeff coaches privately and produces demos so if you get to that point you can work with someone you're familiar with, and more importantly, who's familiar with you.

If you're out there working, you'll be interested in the Advanced Workout with the Pros. Deb Doetzer runs this class, and she's a hoot and a half. Very experienced and always entertaining, you'll learn plenty from her. The school offers this unique opportunity a couple times during the year, and it's a great way to get to know the professionals who will be hiring, directing, and competing with you. Each week a new guest drops by to share his or her insights on the biz and to make you work your little butt off. Guests include ad agency copywriters/producers, VO casting directors, top-level voice talent and recording engineers. I took the class years ago, and I learned more from it than just about any other class I ever took because I was surrounded by people who were better than me. It took some time, but eventually I rose to their level and haven't looked back since. The people I met in this class were responsible for moving my VO career from nonunion to union, and connecting me to the agents I always wanted to be with. If you're serious about VO, this is the class to take.

Another kind of class that might be beneficial to your VO career is an improv class. I say this from experience. Back when I was learning the art of voice over, I found myself stuck in a rut, all of my reads were coming out sounding the same. I had trouble responding to direction, and as a result there was a monotony and inflexibility in my voice work that was holding me back. On a whim I decided to enroll in an improv class. What an eye opener! Improv classes tend to open your mind, they get you thinking about things in ways that you hadn't before. After finishing, I looked at VO scripts much differently, and my reads reflected the results. I started booking more jobs. 'Nuff said. Check out class offerings at The Second City, I.O. Chicago, Comedy Sportz or any of the other improv venues around town.

Print

I can't say much about training to be a print model. The thing is, it's all about how you look. So what it comes down to is this: do you have a look that's marketable and in demand? If you do, you'll work, and if you don't, you won't. In Chicago's acting schools there are no classes for actors wanting to get into print modeling. What's more, those doing the hiring generally won't look for you to be trained.

Many print jobs require actors to show up with a bunch of wardrobe choices, sit in front of a camera for a bit, and smile pretty. An hour or two and you're out of there. Some are more involved, though, like the one I did for a cell phone provider. It required a little more effort on my part. I was supposed to be the owner of a catering company, and the client put together a huge ballroom set for the shoot, complete with extras in the background and fancy linens on the tables. My job was to stand in the middle of this place and look like I was conducting important business using my phone. It's actually pretty challenging to pull off this kind of thing without having any lines to say.

Not surprisingly, the kinds of print jobs that actors usually get require a little acting. There's a photography studio in town that used to do a lot of work for Altoids. Their ads are funky and quirky, and often the model must be able to communicate some kind of emotion that fits the circumstances of the ad. Instead of just smiling pretty, the model has to look triumphant, or confident, or embarrassed. Actors are called in for this kind of thing because they're sometimes better suited to emote than people who work solely in print. That's not to say that models can't come up with a look of contrition, but if the ad calls for a person of average looks who needs to do some emoting, the actors are going to get the call for it. This is where your training as an actor will be useful, yet another benefit of having experience under your belt. Some jobs call for you to actually be able to play a sport, or perform some other action that requires you to be familiar with a game, situation or event. But there's no way to be trained for this except the school of hard knocks. Your agent will have some words of wisdom for you, but other than that, you'll learn on the job. And here's hoping that you work a lot.

Trade Shows/Live Events

Companies hire actors for trade shows and live events because they bring something to the table that otherwise wouldn't be there. Usually, their own employees have great sales skills, or product knowledge, or the ability to talk about the company forever. But it's a rare sales guy or girl who has the whole package: they've got the sales skills, the product knowledge, they're great in front of a live audience, they can spit out a script and consistently time it perfectly, they're cool under pressure, they've got a great personality, and they're not bad to look at, either. Oh, and they want to spend the entire convention doing their shtick at the company booth every day, all day long, without fail. If companies had people like that, they wouldn't need to hire actors - thankfully, they need us pretty badly, and we're happy give them the whole package.

Specific training out there for folks who want to work in trade shows doesn't really exist, but there are certain things that trade show agents look for in the people they represent. First off, most of the people who do trade show work are attractive women. This spotlights a stereotype in the business world, which is that conventions are attended by mostly men, and since they're guys, they'll gravitate toward pretty girls. Thus, pretty girls will generate more sales leads for clients, and ultimately help to sell more stuff. Whether or not this is true, I don't know. A look at some websites of agents that represent trade show talent will make it pretty clear: if you're not a pretty girl or boy, your chances of doing this kind of work are considerably smaller.

But Kathleen Hennon, a Chicago-based actress who's a regular on the trade show scene, says that there's more to being successful than being attractive. "A lot goes into the decision of who to hire for which job, but basically, the client wants to hire people who'll show up for work on time with a good attitude and a smile on their face."

As I mentioned before, there are several ways you can work a trade show. To be a crowd gatherer, you'll need to be willing and able to be on your feet all day. Sales experience is a plus. Your job will be to pull people into the booth to make sure your client is getting as much interaction with the show attendees as possible. When there's a presentation Hennon says, "My job is to sell that seat to you, because your attention is being pulled a million different ways on the show floor."

A host position requires you to be sociable, friendly and outgoing. As a host you might be doing anything from handing out freebies and samples, to doing administrative tasks around the booth like making sure brochures or take-away materials are always in fresh supply.

Product specialists are usually hired by a client for an entire show season, meaning that you'll do a series of shows with them around the country. You'll be trained on their product or service, given scripts, and will be expected to mingle with show goers and help the client develop good business leads and contacts. That's what a trade show is all about, generating prospective customers for the client. You'll go through the scripts in one-on-one interactions. Product specialists need to be well-spoken, intelligent and articulate, and able to handle topical questions while not letting on that they have no real knowledge about their client other than what they learned for the show.

Being a presenter is another way you can work a show. The combination of skills that you need to be a live presenter is pretty unique. To begin with, you can't be queasy about speaking in front of a large audience about something you have little or no knowledge about. Secondly, in my experience, many clients expect that you'll do your presentation using the ear prompter. That's for practicality reasons as much as any other, because frequently the script isn't final until shortly before the show starts. So if you're memorizing the script, you'd be starting over the night before you do your first presentation. Secondly, EARs are important because, often, as you're talking, there's a video or some other multimedia component that's timed to the script. So you need to consistently hit certain spots in the script at certain times, which is tricky without using an EAR. Thirdly, you need to deliver the script with a good amount of your own personality, which has to be pretty mainstream and fit into the client's image. Finally, you've got to be good on the floor as well as on stage. The perception will be that you work for the company for which you're doing the presentation. So when you're done speaking, don't be surprised if audience members want to chat with you. You have to be good with people and good at passing them off to others in the booth who can answer their questions, without letting on that you're not connected with that company at all. My standard line is, "I'm in marketing, let me get you someone who can give you a better answer than I could." Works every time.

Given all you'll need to do as a presenter, you'd do well to take Act One's EAR/Industrial course. If you're not on the EAR, you've got less of a chance of being a live narrator, but if you're hoping to be a presenter without it, then brush up on your memorization skills.

TV/Film

To be considered for TV/film work in Chicago, it's almost a must to be a theater actor. Casting directors in town like to put stage actors on their auditions because they know they've got the chops to get the roles. They can go to your show, see you on stage, and know exactly which roles you'd be right for. If you're not on stage, you won't have that advantage and they'll have to guess at what you can do, making their job more difficult and risky. When they're casting a film or TV project, they're putting their reputation on the line because the producer is counting on them to find the best actors for the role. Understandably, they'd rather bring in actors they know than those they don't.

If this sounds like a catch-22, it is. You can't really make a living in Chicago theater, yet you have to do it if you want a shot at the TV/film roles. Theater in this town carries a lot of weight with everyone from agents to casting directors, and it shows up in the availability of TV/film auditions. There are exceptions, but in general if you're not on stage, you're not going to be considered for that kind of work.

A look at my resume will show that I'm not that heavy into theater. I've explained why, but I haven't explained the cost. As a result of me spending the last decade concentrating on doing the things that will allow me to make a living, and passing on a lot of opportunities in the theater, I'm offered less TV/film auditions than if I had done the opposite. I, along with my agents, have had to spend time and energy convincing the casting directors in town that I'm more than just a commercial and industrial guy. As of this writing we're making progress, but it's still an uphill battle.

What does this mean for you? It means that if you want a shot at the TV/film roles in town, you'll have to incorporate some theater into your career efforts. If you're a seasoned theater actor, this is great news because you now have all the reasons in the world to continue doing what you love. Keep in mind, though, that the fact you do theater does not guarantee you these kinds of auditions, but it does give you a leg up on actors that don't take to the stage often. You'll still need relationships with agents and casting directors to get those appointments. If you're new to the business, this is where your training will be hugely important.

Opportunities for actors just beginning their training abound in Chicago. If you're new to the craft, start with an acting 101 class, such as Acting Studio Chicago's Level I class. There they follow the Shurtleff method as the common thread running through their program. The Shurtleff philosophy is a practical, clear and definitive way to attack scripts. A lot of emphasis is placed on building relationships and finding discoveries in scripts. More advanced actors can take advantage of the school's higher level classes like monologue workshops and cold reading. This might be a good place for actors who have been away from the business for a time. If you've done some acting in the past but it's been a while, hit a cold reading class to jump start your acting gene again.

Actors who are further along in their work would benefit greatly from Kurt Naebig's advanced scene study class at Acting Studio Chicago. Kurt is a notable director and actor in town. He's also a real pro, and has a way of getting his point across productively to students. You'll have to audition to get into his class, which is limited to 12 students. This means you'll be working with high-quality actors doing high quality work. I've learned a lot just by watching other students. Kurt assigns you a scene and a partner, and you'll spend a couple weeks working on it, in and out of class. By the time the course ends you'll probably do three scenes with three different partners.

Act One Studios also offers a full variety of classes for beginners through advanced level actors. Start with Fundamentals I if you're new to the business or it's been a while since you've spoken someone else's words. Script analysis and character development provide the foundation for further study. Act One also provides students with lots of opportunities to perform in front of their peers. At the end of Fundamentals III, students present a scene at an end-of-term showcase. This is a great way for newbies to get used to acting in front of a crowd.

While The Green Room's first three levels in their program focus on commercials, there's more to explore in their upper-level classes, where you'll learn about acting for TV and film, and the specific issues that go along with those media. Their training culminates with students shooting and creating a short film. Check their website for more details.

A Word About Experience

You can't get experience without working, and you can't work without experience. Believe me, everyone in the industry knows this, and if you're just starting out, we all feel your pain. All the training in the world can go out the window when you're in front of a camera on your first job, and there are fifteen lights spotted on you, twenty people standing around watching your every move, and five of them are telling you to move left, look right, tuck your shirt in, don't move your head when you talk, and hold the toothbrush with the bristles facing camera right, not YOUR right. No on camera class can prepare you for that, and only experience will help to calm your nerves during the toughest situations.

When I first started out, I just wanted to do voice overs. I didn't see myself as an actor, because I wasn't interested in being on camera. But wouldn't you know it, my first paying job was a darned on camera job! It was a recruiting video for the University of North Carolina, and I was hired as the host, a college kid who goes to UNC and wants to tell prospective students they should go there, too. As you can imagine, I was terrified. I hadn't even taken an on camera class at that point, but what little experience I had got me hired. In the ten-minute video, the host was only on screen for about one minute. The rest was voice over narration. Since I had just finished a couple months worth of voice over training, I had the most experience as a voice talent of anyone who auditioned for the job. It was just luck that they really needed a voice over guy, not someone who had never worked in front of a microphone before. That person was me.

The job started out really rough. I had three lines to say and for the life of me I couldn't remember them. And when I could, I'd mess them up somehow. I had to say something like "Contact the Student Life Department for more information." I remember saying "info" instead of "information" over and over again. The director finally realized that for whatever reason, I wasn't going to say "information" no matter how many takes she gave me. When the video was finally done, "info" it was.

I was freaked out beyond belief. Here I was, a voice over guy, and they stuck me in front of a camera with all the lights and the people watching and the lines to memorize! My nerves were going strong, and although they didn't take over completely, they were trying really hard to shut my brain down. Inexperience can do that, and the only antidote is experience.

So how do you get some? How do you go about the process of building confidence? Taking classes is a start. After the UNC job, that's exactly what I did. I got myself into an on camera class and began to learn as much about that kind of work as I knew about voice over work.

Back then taking a class was really my only viable option. At that time the availability of home video equipment wasn't like it is now. In the mid-1990s you couldn't get a home video camera for less than a thousand bucks. Since I couldn't afford that, practicing for class involved reading my scripts in front of a mirror. That worked, but what I really wanted was a setup where I could tape myself, watch the result, and experiment with changing things up in the privacy of my own home.

Which brings me to the second way you can get some experience. Today there are video cameras on the market that cost as little as $150, and with a tripod you've got a home studio for under $200. Even cheaper options exist if you buy them on eBay or borrow a camera from someone. Besides paying for time in front of a camera by taking a class, this is the best way to get familiar with performing in front of a lens. However, I'd go with this option in conjunction with a class. The down side to studying on your own at home is that you've got no one but yourself to critique your performance. You probably don't have the knowledge to be able to tell what changes you should make. Or worse, you may *think* you know what to change. Supplement the self-teaching method by enrolling in a course that will do you some good.

Taking a class or buying a camera to use at home are better ways of gaining experience than learning on the set. Certainly you're going to learn a lot more from a job than you can from a class, but that's not the best place to learn. Some people (myself included) have picked up much of what they know in the natural course of working. Directors, other actors, and even crew members can provide a wealth of information and helpful tips that you can sock away in your mind and keep for later, but you want to have at least a little working knowledge before you get cast in a paying job. The key word there is "paying".

Many actors think of the theater as a place to experiment and learn, but it's not a good idea to apply that logic to your time in front of a camera. By the time you're on the set shooting, months (sometimes longer) have gone into planning the job and writing the script. Concepts were pitched, several versions of the script were written, locations were scouted, props were collected, wardrobe was chosen, auditions were held, and lots of money was spent. Very often the budget is so tight that everything absolutely must go according to plan. An eight-hour day just can't stretch into ten hours, because there's no money left to pay for overtime. As actors, it's our job to make sure we don't do anything to stretch out the length of the job. That means that we're expected to show up on time, know our stuff, and do our job well. Understandably, no one wants to pay you to learn on their set. They expect you to know what you're doing before they hire you. After all, that's why they hired you - because in the audition you looked like you knew what you were doing! It's a cruddy feeling when you're totally lost on a set and you know you're getting paid anyway. Solve that problem by getting comfortable in class and practicing at home to get sharp.

The great thing about taking classes is that you're not just going to learn about the subject being taught, you're also going to pick up bits and pieces about other aspects of the business. Invariably the subject of agents, headshots, voice demos, and other industry-related stuff will come up for discussion. Depending on who you hear it from, the information could be spot on accurate or horribly off track. I'm here to make sure you get the right information. Up next: things every working actor can't live without.

CHAPTER FIVE

Headshots and Resumes - The Chicago Way

Y ou have a job to do, and you need the tools to do it. A few things are an absolute must in this business: a headshot, a resume and an agent. Without these three things, your chances of acting for a living are about as good as your chances of becoming the next Pope.

The Headshot

We in the industry don't like to admit this, but how you look is integral to the kind of career you'll develop. There's work for everyone, from the drop-dead beautiful to the creepy, and your headshot is your only way of showing people which category you fit into. It's been called the actor's calling card, but really it's the actor's lifeline to the professionals who'll be making decisions about you. Agents, casting directors and producers will all make different judgments about you based on your headshot, which makes it the single most important tool in any actor's tool belt.

For years the standard in Chicago had been the 8x10 black and white headshot on matte paper. Color shots now rule the land. If you were in this business back in the days of black and white, and you're thinking about getting back in using the same old headshot, forget it. The shot that once got you a ton of auditions will make you look irrelevant and out of touch today. Get a new one. The price of admission to every agent, casting director, audition and ultimately every job, will be a headshot. Since you only have one chance to make an impression on these decision makers, your headshot should be attention-grabbing at the very least. If you don't already know what constitutes a good headshot, you can check out mine at www.chrisagos.com. There are also lots of websites that'll give you an idea, but it comes down to this: does it look like you as you appear in real life, and does the image draw the viewer in and make them want to call you in?"

The most important thing about a headshot is that it looks like you. Not the person that you hope to be some day, or the person that you really wish you were, but the person that you actually are right now. If you're a dark and mysterious-looking thirty something, yet your headshot makes you look like a bright, bubbly twenty-five year old, a casting director will be very disappointed when you walk into their office. Why? They need a bubbly twenty something to do their job, not someone who's ten years older and looks it in real life.

Your headshot should not only look like you, but it should also be compelling. It should convey something about your personality. It's not enough to sit in front of a camera and have someone take your picture. That's what you do when you get your driver's license. A step up from that are the class pictures we take of our kids every year in school. They're a nice record of what children look like from year-to-year, but I bet you never looked at one of them and said, "Wow! She looks like she'd be really good at comedy!" You want your headshot to convey certain qualities about your personality that are not immediately obvious, and by that I mean that everything about the shot has to add up to a complete package that describes who you are. Your choice of clothing, makeup, hairstyle, jewelry (or lack thereof), background, body language, facial expression and lighting will all combine to convey a message about what kinds of roles you can play. Going to a headshot photographer is the only way you'll be able to make that message clear in one, carefully calculated shot.

Your Photographer

Who you choose as your photographer will have a great impact on how your shots look. Getting a good headshot out of an actor is a combination of art and science, and good shooters have it figured out. You should interview a couple before you choose which one you think will do the best job for you. Almost all photographers offer free no-obligation consultations. Make a few appointments, and when you're in their studio, take a look at the work they've done. Look to see if there's variety in their work, or if all their headshots tend to look the same. See if they make their subjects look happy, sexy, mysterious, dreamy, commanding or contemplative. While you're there poking around, take note of not only the obvious things like their price list and turnaround time (the time between when they shoot you and when you can get your prints), but also the general feel of the place. Do you get good vibes? Were you greeted with a pleasant smile when you came in the door? Do the photographer and his staff seem to care about how you're feeling as you move around the studio? Do they make you feel welcome? Is there an air of brisk activity about the place or stifled boredom? Does the studio seem well organized or chaotic? And while you're at it, were you able to find a parking space? Can you bring your own music to play during the shoot? Also, use the bathroom while you're there, or check out the dressing room if there is one – are they bright, clean and well cared for? All of these issues will come together for you on the day of your shoot, and any of them could affect how you feel, and thus influence the result of your shots.

While all of these things are good to take stock of, the most important factor in choosing a shooter is how easily you interact with him or her. If you don't get along with your photographer, it doesn't matter if you've walked into the cleanest, peppiest, most well run photography studio in the city. More than anything you want to feel comfortable in front of the camera, which means that you want to feel comfortable with the person creating your images. There are shooters out there who lack people skills and are all business during a shoot. They can put together a technically solid shot that's in focus and has good composition, but they lack the ability to get interesting results from their subjects. The best photographers are able to not only construct a technically good shot, but also pull out the best looks from their actors. A good photographer should also be willing to work with your ideas about the shot. Avoid shooters who are pushy and believe their way is the only way. You should choose someone you could easily hang out with who runs a place you'd like to hang out in. If you can find that, then you'll be able to open up in front of the camera and produce some really great results. Your mood will be affected by the entire experience, not just by one aspect of it.

Finding photographers is really easy. Start by Googling "Chicago headshot photographers". All of them have sites with galleries full of sample shots. When you come across a couple you really like, set up appointments and go for a visit. Don't be put off if you find a couple shooters that don't have studios of their own. There are some really talented people out there who are one-man or -woman shops and don't have permanent studio space. If you're considering one of these folks, you might do your consultation over coffee. At the very least, chat with them on the phone before you book a session with them. Don't ever hire your headshot photographer after exchanging a few emails, because if you get to the session and find that you don't like the person, you're screwed, and your shots will show it.

A more interesting method of finding a photographer is to visit the websites of agents in town and browse through their talent galleries. When you find a few shots you like, write a short email to one of the agents politely asking which photographer took which shot. Something like this should get a reply: "Hi, I'm an actor looking to get some new headshots and I found a couple on your site that I really like. Would you be able to tell me whom Susan Smith and Daniel Davis used for their shots? I'd appreciate knowing which shooters in town do good work. Thanks in advance for a reply!" The agent should eventually get back to you. If they don't, either email another one in the agency, or wait a week or two before emailing again. Be persistent without being a hassle. This method does a couple of things: not only does it let you find out who did those shots, but you'll also likely discover who that agent likes to recommend to their talent. If agents are sending their actors to a shooter, the shooter gets good results. And the best part is, you're introducing yourself to an agent, and that could be useful down the road.

The most obvious way to find a good shooter is to ask other actors who they used, but this only works if you have actor friends, you're in a class or are out there auditioning. At auditions, actors have their shots in their hands as they wait to go into the audition room. When you get a look at one you like, quickly and discreetly ask who shot it. You want to get some information, but you don't want to distract the other actor from preparing for the audition. Some people don't like to chat before going into the room. Something like "Hey, love your shots. Who did them?" is quick enough that you won't get a dirty look for being annoying. This will get you a name, which you can look up later online. If you're in a class, chat all you want with other actors about their shots. If you're out and about auditioning, working and taking classes, just ask around. The best recommendations come from word of mouth.

The Shoot

Once you've found someone you think is the best fit for you, it's time to schedule your session's date and time. You'll want to think about this a little, because it's not just a matter of when you and the photographer are both available. Consider what time of day you feel and look your best. Some people are early risers; some are night people. I tend to think more clearly in the morning, but I seem to look better in the afternoon, so I try to book my sessions after two or three o'clock. When selecting a date, try to make sure that you have nothing else to do on that day. This can't always happen, but the idea is to keep the day as stress-free as possible. If you share a car with someone, avoid scheduling your session when they might need to use it in case the shoot goes late or your car doesn't show up when you need it. Try to pick a day when you know things at work will be predictable and relatively relaxed. And if you're dealing with any personal issues like an illness in the family or marriage troubles, do your best to avoid combining those with your headshot session. You shouldn't go directly from your therapist to your photographer's studio, nor should you drop your mom off for some outpatient surgery and then run off to get your headshots done. You want your mind to be as quiet and clear as it can be when you're in front of that lens. Do your best to pick a time when you can be mentally and emotionally unaffected by your life's circumstances.

Let's say that on the day of your shoot you're able to sleep in a little later than normal. You leave with plenty of time to get to the studio. When you arrive for your session you're able to park easily. You're greeted warmly and feel welcomed by the photographer, and are shown into the clean and well-lit dressing room so you can spread your stuff out and select what you're going to wear. Someone hits "play" on the music you brought. You spend a little time joking around with your photographer while you choose your wardrobe. You're offered something to drink, you have plenty of time to get the session done, you're happy and healthy, and you look it. That'll come through in your shots. In contrast, if you can't find parking and you dash in and people are ticked off that you're late, and they rush you into their crappy dressing room, you're forced to listen to their crappier music, and during the shoot the photographer seems grumpy and disorganized, that's not going to be good for your shots. The stress you're under will come through loud and clear, and you won't like the result.

A friend of mine once told me about an experience he had with a photographer that came highly recommended by his agent. He scheduled a consultation and it went well enough that he decided to hire the photographer. On the day of the shoot my friend showed up on time, but the photographer wasn't ready for him. He had not begun setting up his studio for the session, so my friend had to wait an hour and a half before the first frame was shot. After a few test shots, the lighting had to be adjusted, which accounted for more waiting time. On top of this, the shooter was a big talker and told lots of stories, eating up time and not getting a lot done. Ordinarily this wouldn't have been a big problem, except that on that particular day my friend had a voice over job after the shoot. The session took over four hours to complete, much longer than it should take to get a decent headshot, and by the time it was over my friend was frustrated, late for his job, and felt like he just wasted his time and money. Those frustrations showed up in his headshots, and after trying them out for a couple of months, he decided to scrap them. They weren't getting him the work they should because the overall message that his shots conveyed about him was that he was a negative, stressed-out guy, which is something he's not in real life.

On the other end of the spectrum, there are photographers who will go out of their way to make sure you get the best shots possible. These are the professionals who make the sessions all about the actor, not about the photographer. They're the ones who ask you what you want, and then give it to you. You want to look like a vixen from the 1940s? You got it. You need to look tough and dirty, yet sensitive and educated? No problem. The good shooters know that your livelihood depends on the end result.

Policies and procedures differ with every shooter, but generally things work like this: after your session is finished, you'll get thumbnails of the session. Every frame that was taken at your shoot will either be posted online or given to you on a DVD. You might have 100 or even 400 images. Get comfortable in front of your computer, and take a good look at all of them. Pick out a couple that you like the best – remember, you're looking for the shots that best express who you are – then get outside opinions. If possible, get someone in the business to look at them. Get a teacher, another actor, or better yet an agent if you already have one, to give you their honest opinion about which shot or shots you should choose. Once you have a few contenders, follow the shooter's procedures for getting larger prints. Sometimes the photographer will include a certain number of 8x10s in the price of the session, and if you want to see more than that, you'll have to pay extra for them. This is absolutely worth the cost, because sometimes there are more than a few really good shots, and you don't want to miss them by trying to save money. So get as many 8x10s as you think it'll take for you to pick the one or ones you want to use. Then pass those around to the people you trust and get their opinion a second time.

A word of warning here: family members (especially mothers) usually love whatever you put in front of them. If they love you, they'll love any headshot of you and thus aren't good sources for unbiased opinions. You want to have someone with a bit of a critical eye look at your shots. Your photographer might be one person you could ask for advice. Most of them have plenty of experience to back up their opinion; so don't be afraid to ask them what they think, too.

When you've settled on one or two shots as the final choices, you'll have to get them duplicated. You'll hand out a couple headshots every time you try to get an agent or go to an audition, so you're going to need a lot of them. Because I have an established career, I start with 250 copies of each shot I choose. I'll go through those pretty quickly and I place reorders of 100 at a time when I need them. If you're just starting out, you might start with 100 prints. There are several reputable companies in Chicago that duplicate headshots and any one of them do good work. Look them up on Yelp.com to get other actors' opinions of them. I work with a duplication house in Los Angeles called Argentum Photo, which I highly recommend. Ask your shooter who they'd suggest. In any case, you should have your prints within two weeks of picking out the final shots.

By the time you're done hiring a photographer and reproducing the prints, you should expect to spend somewhere between $500 and $700 before your headshots are ready to be seen by the industry. That doesn't include extras like hiring a hair and makeup stylist ($75-$150), paying the photographer a little extra to travel to a location you want to shoot in ($100-$250), additional 8x10s ($10-$25 each), retouching your images ($100-$200 each image) or buying clothes specifically for your shoot (sky's the limit).

My Uncle Harry Has A Nice Camera...

If you're wondering whether it's worth it to spend that kind of money on a headshot, here's your answer: even if you just want to try out acting on a short term basis, you absolutely cannot get away with cutting corners on your headshot. There are lots of reasons why, but the biggest issue is credibility. You have to look like you know what you're doing, even if you don't know anything at all. Otherwise, you won't even get in the door.

When an agent holds your headshot in his or her hand, she'll only hold it for about three seconds. That's how long you'll have to make the kind of impression you want to make. During that time the agent will make judgments about how old you are and your type. If they're even remotely interested in who they see staring back at them, they'll flip the shot over and look at your resume. Depending on what they see there, and after determining if you'd be a good fit for their agency, they'll either drop your shot on a pile of other headshots or they'll throw it away. And then they'll pick up someone else's shot and repeat the process, perhaps hundreds of times that day. So imagine having a headshot that looks like it was taken by your uncle in his basement. It would make you look like you have no idea what you're doing. That might be the case, but we don't want anyone to know that just by glancing at your headshot. Give yourself the best chance to succeed and hire a real photographer who knows the deal. It'll be well worth the expense.

I've worked with some great shooters over the years, and they're listed at the end of this chapter. Each of them has done headshots for me at one point or another. None of them paid me for my endorsement. Just check out their websites and interview a couple of them. Each has their strengths, and any one of them will give you great service at a fair price. One of these shooters could be a good match for you, but if you don't click with one on the list, search online and follow the suggestions I've outlined.

Younger Performers

A word about headshots for kids: if you have a child actor in the house and you're thinking that you can get away with using a school picture as a headshot, forget it. At very young ages, like from birth to about three or four years, snapshots are just fine because babies grow and change so quickly. Professionally produced headshots should be considered by the age of five or six. As for teenagers, don't rely on those senior pictures that high school kids take when they're graduating. People who look at headshots all day every day will pick those out in a second and toss them into the circular file.

The Resume

You've got your great headshot. Now you've got to tell people what you've been up to; even if the answer to that is absolutely nothing related to acting, you'll need a resume to give people some idea of who you are and how they can use you. Your headshot makes the first impression, and your resume can help seal the deal.

In Chicago, resumes are printed on a piece of paper that's trimmed to the size of your 8x10 headshot. I take a stack of plain white printer paper to FedEx Office and have them use their flat cutter to trim the whole stack down to 8x10. Then, using my laser printer at home, I print resumes as I need them. I staple the resume to my headshot back to back, so that the viewer can look at the image on one side and flip the shot over to read the resume on the other side. Two staples at the top take care of it. This allows someone to easily remove my resume from the headshot and send it through a fax machine if they want to. Don't use glue, tape, or more staples than you need. Glue wrinkles paper, tape makes it look like a kindergarten project, and why on Earth would you want to put more holes in your beautiful, painstakingly crafted headshot than necessary? The idea is to make the whole thing look clean and professional.

Do's And Don'ts

Before we talk about what to put on your resume, let's take a second to talk about what not to do. It's tempting, especially if you don't have a lot of experience, to fill up empty space on your resume with all kinds of crap. Clip art, funny sayings, jokes and drawings make you look like someone who has no interest in, or idea of how to be professional. Resumes are important tools to everyone involved in the process. They're important to you because they help you get in the running for work, and they're important to the agent or casting director because they use them to see if you fit the current job they're working. Finally, the client needs them because they want to know that you can do the job if they hire you. On a typical day all of these people could look at hundreds of headshots and resumes before they eat lunch. They don't have a lot of free time and distracting them with goofy stuff will just tick them off and earn your headshot a spot in their trashcan.

Another thing to avoid is putting your personal contact information directly on the resume. Phone numbers and email addresses can go on a cover letter if you're submitting your shot to a decision maker, but they should be kept off the resume itself. You want to keep a lid on your privacy. When your headshot and resume are floating around out there in the world, you've got no control over where it winds up. Who's to say that some creep might get his hands on it? Maybe he'll think he can harass you in some way, or even show up where you live. It's happened before, so just keep it in mind. If you've got an acting website with demos and reels posted, the web address is okay to include, but keep the personal stuff private. The only contact information that should be permanently placed on the resume is your agent's when you have one.

Ok, enough of the don'ts. What about the do's? Resumes are the actor's only immediate lifeline to the decision makers. Headshots are the attention getters, but resumes are the substance. So we've got to give them something to look at: something honest, productive and compelling.

It's easier for me to show you some resumes than to simply talk about them. A long time ago I started saving my resumes, so that one day I could look back and see what kind of progress I made in my career. Turns out that I never looked at them until I thought to include them here, but I'm glad I kept them because they're going to be very educational. Here's my very first resume, reproduced exactly as it appeared on the back of my first headshot. I put it together with the help of two books, one on acting and one on writing resumes to get your first job.

Chris Agos

8S251 Palomino Dr
Naperville, IL 60540
(312)513-8251

Age:23
Height/Weight: 5'10"/185
Hair/Eyes: Blonde/Brown

EDUCATION

DePaul University, Chicago, IL
Bachelor of Science, expected February, 1996

Naperville North High School, Naperville, IL
Class of 1990

INDUSTRIAL
FILMS

-"Kevin Gets A Clue", Kevin, Nalco Chemical, Naperville, IL 1995

INDUSTRY
EXPERIENCE

-Chorus Member, "Don Giovanni", DePaul University, Chicago, IL,
    1995
-Chorus Member, "Carmen", DePaul University, Chicago, IL,
    1994
-Baritone, The Belden Carolers, an a capella Christmas caroling
    quartet featured during private parties and on WGN
    Morning News, December 1994
-Baritone, DePaul University Chamber Choir, DePaul University,
    Chicago, IL 1992-1995
-Supporting Lead Role, Lucian P. Smith, "The Boys Next Door",
    College of DuPage, Lombard, IL 1991
-Lead Role, Billy Crocker, "Anything Goes", Naperville North
    High School, Naperville, IL 1990

VOICE OVERS

-"Kevin Gets A Clue", Kevin, Nalco Chemical, Naperville, IL 1995

SPECIFIC
TRAINING

-Voice Over Training with Ray Van Steen, Chicago, IL 1995
-Classical Voice Study, American Conservatory of Music
    Chicago, IL 1990-1991

INTERESTS

Rollerblading – Tennis – Archery – Football – Mountain Biking
Painting – Traveling – Watch Collecting
Gardening – Art Collecting

Looking at this, you can tell right away that this is the resume of someone who doesn't have a ton of experience in acting, let alone writing resumes. The formatting is straight out of a classic business resume book and isn't appropriate for an acting resume. There's a lot of extraneous information, but there are a few relevant items: the industrial, which I also turned into a voiceover job, the voiceover training and the shows. All the other stuff is just filler, but it's what I had at the time. Resumes that have little to report are fine and actually expected since everyone has to start somewhere, but following the industry standard for showing your work is a must. Don't use my first resume as an example. Here's what's wrong with it, starting at the top:

1. I put my home address and phone number on there! A no-no for sure.
2. There's no need to put your age on your resume. Let whomever is looking at your headshot decide how old you look.
3. The height, weight, and physical features are okay, but I forgot to include my suit size. Women should include their dress size.
4. Education is important, but not the most important bit of information on the resume. Any kind of industry experience should go first, divided into categories. Education goes at the bottom, but only if it's industry-specific, interesting or the only thing you've got.
5. I should have left out the title and geographic location of the industrial. This is true for all job categories.
6. I went crazy with formatting. The underlining, quotes, dates and bullets are unnecessary.
7. The training section is okay, except for the dates, which don't need to be included.
8. The "Interests" category should be called "Special Skills/Interests".

We can make this resume a lot better, starting by moving things around. When an agent or casting director is considering your resume, they're more likely glancing at it than studying it. To make it easier to read, I'm going to put the categories in the center of the page and center the information underneath them. It's easier on the eyes. People who are interested enough to look at what's on the other side of your headshot really just want to know what work you've done and where you've done your training.

Education is really secondary to work experience. So, let's move the education section down to the bottom, above the "Interests" section.

We'll replace the top section with one called "Theater", since I had more of those credits than anything else. There I'll list my college shows and the one show I did in high school. Actually, because at the time I was a young guy, putting a few more high school productions down wouldn't be a bad thing. At least it shows that I have had a long-standing interest in acting.

I'll display the listings following the industry standard, which is show title, role and theater company. I'll cut out the two singing groups because they don't have anything to do with acting. I'll leave the industrial job, but reorganize the information to follow the industry format (client, role and production company).

Moving down, I'll leave the voice over job as is, except for a format change. I'll call the next category "Training" instead of specific training. Next we have the education information that we moved down, and finally the last section will be given a name change to be a little more descriptive. Now it looks like this:

CHRIS AGOS

<u>Height: 5'10</u>   <u>Weight: 185</u>   <u>Eyes:Brown</u>   <u>Hair:Blonde</u>   <u>Suit: 42R</u>

THEATER

The Boys Next Door	Lucien	College of DuPage
Don Giovanni	Chorus	DePaul University
Carmen	Chorus	DePaul University
Anything Goes	Billy	Naperville North HS
West Side Story	Riff	Naperville North HS
Brigadoon	Tommy	Naperville North HS

INDUSTRIAL FILMS

Nalco Chemical	College Student	Nalco Productions

VOICE OVERS

Nalco Chemical	Narrator	Nalco Productions

TRAINING

Voice Over Training: Classical Voice Study:
Ray Van Steen   Amer. Conservatory of Music
    Range: Baritone

EDUCATION

DePaul University, Chicago, IL
Bachelor of Science, expected Feb. 1996

Naperville North High School, Naperville, IL
Class of 1990

SPECIAL SKILLS/INTERESTS

Good with Kids – Tennis – Archery – Biking – Cooking – Traveling – Knuckle Cracking

Pretty cool, huh? This is a resume I would have been proud to hand out at that point in my career. It clearly and honestly spells out what I've been up to, and reads like it belongs to someone who's on the right road. There's some training, there's some work experience, and there's some history of being on stage, even though the productions were at school. In an agent's mind, these things add up to someone who might be new, but has done some research and is willing to take the steps necessary to advance his career. Before they meet you, that's all the agent can really ask for.

Enough about me, let's work with your resume. If you've got some training and work behind you already, skip the next paragraph. This one's for those with no experience at all.

Relax. No one's born with a fantastic resume filled with impressive credits. Everyone has to start at a point where it's obvious you've never done one bit of professional acting. That's ok, and expected by the decision makers. If you look at my first resume, you'll see that there's only one real job to speak of, the one for Nalco Chemical, which I conveniently turned into two jobs by listing it under both the industrial and voice over categories. It's there because I managed to luck into it before I even had a headshot or resume. If I had put together a resume before working that job, it wouldn't have been listed at all and the resume would have only contained the shows I did in school and my training. If you're just beginning your career, you've probably taken at least one class of some kind (acting, improv, dance, voice, etc.) and/or been in some kind of production (school, community theater, children's theater, etc.) Feel free to list as many of those credits as you'd like, because right now they're all you have to include. Start with the ones that seem the most professional. Productions you worked on in college probably outrank any community theater you've done. If you're going to list video/film credits, student work counts for a lot if it's part of a curriculum in a well-respected college or university. You and your buddies messing around with a home video camera doesn't count as work. Leave it off unless the film has been accepted into film festivals. If you've been in videos at work, like sales videos, list them as industrial work. Be careful with voiceover work, though. If you've got a radio show on any size AM/FM station or on the Web, that's resume worthy. But if you do live announcing for the local high school football game, or are a reader in your church, leave it off. It's not going to be relevant to anyone in the acting world.

The question you have to ask about each credit is this: does it directly and obviously relate to the kind of work I'm now going after? If the answer is honestly no (like emceeing a non-profit's fund raiser), then leave it off. It's better to have few to no real credits than a resume filled with irrelevant items. If you've got nothing to list, get into an acting class. I don't care what kind – just take one that excites you. And finally, if you're tempted to make something up, don't. It'll come back to bite you in the worst way, and you won't recover from it. Would you really want your career sunk before it even starts? Keep it real.

Impress Them Early

No matter what kind of experience you have, you always want to list the most impressive credit on your resume first, right at the top. By impressive, I mean the hardest kind of work to get. In Chicago, that usually means film or TV work. List the most recognizable, and/or most viewed thing you've done within that category first, followed by the rest. That goes for each category with a couple of exceptions noted below.

Deciding which categories to list can depend on what kind of work you're going after. For a while I had several different resumes: one for TV/film, one for theater, one for trade shows, and one for industrials. Depending on what kind of audition I was going on, I'd give them the one that had the emphasis on that kind of work. Nowadays, I only use one resume. This is what it looks like:

Chris Agos

SAG, AFTRA

Stewart Talent 312.943.3131 • www.chrisagos.com

Height: 5'10"   Weight: 165   Eyes: Brown   Hair: Dk. Blond   Suit: 40R

T V

Ride-Along	co-starring	dir: Michael Offer/Fox
The Beast	co-starring	dir: Christine Moore/A&E
A Moving Experience (pilot)	Host	dir: Dan Lombardi/HGTV
Nano U	Host	Big Ten Network

Theater

Pacific	Robert (und.)	Steppenwolf Garage
The Lonesome West	Father Welsh	Buffalo Theatre Ensemble
Standing On My Knees	Robert	Janus Theatre Company
Jekyll & Hyde	Spider	Jedlicka Perf Arts Center.

Industrials

Roserem	Heidelberg	Sears
Cook Biotech	Dremel	Ford
McDonald's	Monsanto	IBM
EAS/Body For Life	Walgreens	NYSE
American Forces Network	Xtra Lease	iRacing.com
Snap-On Tools	Beneful	State Farm
Anheuser Busch	Brunswick	Die Hard
American Heart Assn.	Novartis	Grainger
Takeda Pharmaceuticals	Nutrilite	Teradata
True Value Hardware	Allstate	Boeing

Voice Over

Chrysler	Corona	Ford
Molson	MGD 64	Nike
Pepto Bismol	Subway	Chevy
Sea World	Philip Morris	Hoover
Delta Airlines	Autolite Spark Plugs	Bob Evans
National Geographic	Coors Light	Stelara
Western Union	United Airlines	Cadillac
LifeFitness	Genworth Financial	Budweiser

Commercials

Leo Burnett, Mullen, DraftFCB, Eicoff, JWT Detroit, Y&R, Doner, Partners+Simons, Osborn&Barr, Hoffman-Lewis, Euro RSCG, Allen & Gerritsen, Red212

Live Events

Toyota	Presenter	WIRED NextFest
Panasonic	Presenter	CES
Crest	Presenter	ADA
Heidelberg	Presenter	Graph Expo
Motorola	Presenter	Supercomm, Interop

Education/Training

Bachelor of Science, DePaul University   Master's Class, Jane Alderman   Master's Class, Steve Scott

Special Skills/Interests

EAR, Irish dialect, Father of twins, Good "real person" hands, Tennis, Cooking, Knuckle cracking

You can use this resume as a template for yours, but let me explain some of the choices I made and why. First, the information at the top is pretty standard: name, unions, agent contact information, and website. If you're not in a union, don't put "nonunion", or "pre-union", just leave it blank. Same if you're Taft-Hartley for a union. If you don't know what that means, I'll discuss it later in the chapter on unions. For now, unless there's a union card in your wallet, don't list anything. The website is there if people want to view my reels. Next up are the physical stats, which should always be near the top of any acting resume. If you're a singer and are looking to capitalize on that, list your range here. I'm not going after musicals so I left mine off. And then we get to the good stuff.

TV

I put TV first, and listed my most recent and most recognizable credit at the top. If I had film work worth putting on a resume, I'd list it here as well, but I don't. I've done independent films that have never seen the light of day, but those aren't going to help my cause, they'll just raise some suspicions that I'm making the credit up. So I leave them off because they're not beneficial.

Theater

This category holds a lot of weight with decision makers in town. Chicago has a very active theater scene, and people want to know that you've played your part in it. I've already talked about how I don't do a lot of it, but what I have done is listed with the same system: put either the biggest-name theater company first, or the role that got you the most recognition first.

Industrials

Industrials follow theater. As you can see, this is an area of strength for me. Because of the volume of work that I've done, I can get away with listing just the name of the company who hired me for each project. These items are listed in no particular order because there are so many big corporate names that it really didn't matter what came first, so I positioned them in the most visually pleasing way. Besides, there's really no need to prioritize them because there's hardly an industrial project out there that's ever going to be recognizable to the decision makers. If you don't have a ton of credits, you should follow the standard way of listing an industrial job: company name, role and production company. Like this:

Industrials	Lockjaw Cola	Distributor	Mayhem Productions
	SofTech	Geek	Promise Media
	ValueStore	Associate	North/South, Inc.
	Happy Burger	Narrator	Happy Burger In-House

Voice Over

Following that is voice over work. There are some people who would tell you not to include VO work because it has little to do with acting. I guess I can see their point, but I would disagree that it's not acting, and I include it because it gets me more work than I would if it wasn't there. It's true that many professional actors don't rely on VO work to make money, and as such, they don't bother letting people know they can do it. That's fine for them, but for me, and I hope for you, it's a big part of my career and leaving it out would be foolish. So those credits are there, and

I listed them like I did the industrials, in no particular order. Follow the "impressive first" strategy here if you have few credits. If you've got two or three jobs for lesser-known companies and one from a big name, list the big one first. Also, once you've got a good mix of VO work under your belt, you can list the credits under subcategories like "spots" and "narration". You can just list the companies you worked for, no need to follow the "spot, role, production company" format. It may look like this:

| Voice Overs | Spots: | Collision Pros | Aliant Communications | Travel Adventures |
| | Narration: | Bench Fitness | Good Sam. Hospital | Conservation Trust |

This does a couple of things. First, it tells decision makers that not only can you do VO work, but you're versatile, too. If someone's looking at you for an on camera industrial that happens to have a lot of VO in the script, they'll know that you can handle the job. Secondly, this can be a nice way to spread the work out on the page a little more and take up more space. When you have only a few credits you'll be longing for ways to legitimately fill up the blank space, and this is one way to do it.

Commercials

Under VO is the commercials category. Unless you work in the advertising industry, you're unlikely to recognize any of the names there. That's because I listed the advertising agencies that I've worked for instead of the brands or products I was pitching in the spots. This is the best approach, since it prevents someone from seeing what you've been selling on-air, and deciding that they don't want to use you based on what you've done in the past.

Imagine this scenario: Tide is looking for someone to be in their new series of spots and you're called in to audition. You're given a script, you work hard on it, and you nail it at the audition. You feel great about your chances, and then you never hear anything from Tide again. Then, a month later you're watching your favorite TV show and you see the spot for which you auditioned! And the actor they went with looks just like you! And read the script just like you did! And why the heck was it that actor and not you because you did the same darn thing? There are a thousand answers to that question, but one of the most obvious ones is that you listed a credit for Cheer detergent on your resume. The decision makers probably liked what they saw in your audition, and would have brought you back in for a callback, except for the little detail that you've worked for one of Tide's competitors. Now, it doesn't matter how long ago you worked for Cheer, or that you didn't have a line in the Cheer spot, or (worst of all) that you were an extra in the spot. All Tide knows is that they don't want to hire anyone who's appeared in one of their competitors' ads.

Is this legal? Can Tide do that? Yes. In fact, it's sometimes applied by the unions as a rule called exclusivity. In the chapter on unions I'll explain that in further detail. But is it right? Well, yes and no depending on your point of view. The decision maker's position is that Tide wouldn't want your face associated with their product if it's already associated with a competing product. This makes sense, so you can't really blame them for ruling you out on the grounds that you worked for Cheer. The actor's position is more like this: "Hey, that Cheer spot aired a long time ago. It hasn't seen the light of day since the Clinton administration. The public would never in a million years connect me with both Tide and Cheer, so you're preventing me from making a living without any justification." All that might be true, but in the fast-paced world of casting, they have no way of knowing how old the Cheer spot is, and certainly aren't going to take the time to find out. They have literally hundreds of other people who can take your place on the audition schedule, so it's much easier to just take you off the list. And this is assuming you got to audition in the first place. Having Cheer on your resume might prevent you from even being called in for the first audition. So the solution to that problem is to leave the product and company names off of your credits and replace them with the ad agencies that hire you.

You might have noticed that I didn't apply this logic to the voice over category. That's because you don't hand out headshots and resumes at these auditions. So those decision makers don't have any idea of your work history. Even though it does happen sometimes, it's pretty unlikely that you'll be considered for VO work by the people who hire you for on camera work, so feel free to tell the world for whom you've done voice work.

Live Events

This is a catchall term for anything you were hired to do as a professional actor or presenter in front of a live audience, besides theater. This could include trade shows, auto shows, corporate events like meetings or other gatherings, medical training sessions, or work at theme parks or on cruise ships. If it's related to the kind of work you'd like to pursue, go ahead and include it. All of my credits happen to be trade shows, and since I only have room for a few, I picked the ones that demonstrate some diversity in subject matter. One look at the list tells a decision maker that I can talk about toothpaste as intelligently as technology. This helps to make sure that I'm considered for as much of this kind of work as possible.

Training & Special Skills/Interests

Finally we're down to the more personal categories: Training and Special Skills/Interests. This is your chance to shine a little, and brag about what you're up to in your daily life. For training, I've listed out my undergrad degree, even though it's not an acting degree, and a couple classes that were taught by well-respected, recognizable teachers here in town. Some folks will tell you not to bother listing your degree if it's got nothing to do with acting. I disagree and feel like I worked hard for it, so I should be able to include it. Also, because of my background in the sciences, I get a lot of work that covers medical or otherwise scientific language. So from a professional standpoint, it makes sense to include it.

The special skills section is where you get to have some fun and really make it your own. There's no format to follow other than to make it a short list of things you do well. This is a chance to tell people who you really are, however briefly. Whatever you're good at, include it here. If you're big into martial arts, put it down. If you're a fire eater, list it. If you've swum the English Channel or hold the world record for cramming the highest number of packing peanuts up your nose, make darn sure that's on there. I lead a particularly average life, as you can tell from my list, but I include practical things that might be useful to a production. Maybe there's a production company out there who's developing a cooking show for kids. Or a producer might be looking for guys who play tennis. I'm in the running for those if they come up. It's a good idea to have a few practical things and at least one wacky thing. My list clearly shows that I'm proficient on the ear prompter and TelePrompTer, that I can do a few various things that could be useful, and that if you really need someone to crack his knuckles on demand, I'm your guy. That isn't there because I actually think it's going to get me work, but because it's memorable, and a huge part of the acting game is getting people to remember you. Besides, it's a good conversation starter. I get asked about it once in a while and crack away to their amazement.

You should only include stuff you can actually do. If you ski, but only on the bunny hill and you fall face first every other run, you don't really ski. At least you probably couldn't do it take after take. Be honest with yourself and with the decision makers because if you say you can drive that 5-speed, but end up shredding the transmission in the hero car on the set, you'll experience the wrath of everyone associated with that job from beginning to end: your agent, the casting director, the producer, director, ad agency and their client. Not worth it. Be honest and get the work you should be getting.

A No-No

Speaking of being honest, allow me to sound off on a subject that sends me into fits of consternation. I'm occasionally asked to look at resumes by actors of all experience levels. I'm happy to give my opinion, and it makes me feel good if I can help someone increase his or her chances of getting work. Yet more often than not I see credits that just don't make sense when I consider the actor who handed me the resume. Credits that I'm sure the actor didn't get. This doesn't mean the actor's lying, it just means the he or she is clueless and motivated by a need to look good.

If you've been an extra (sometimes called a background player) in a commercial, film or TV show, that is NOT resume worthy. I know you think that it is, but you're wrong. Here's why: Anyone who fills out an information card and sends in a snapshot can be an extra. My 93-year-old grandmother, who lives in Greece and has zero acting experience, training or even interest, can be an extra if she wants. If you can show up to work on time and bring some wardrobe options with you, you can be an extra.

This does not make you an actor. I'm not saying it's not legitimate hard work. Back in the day, I sat around plenty of holding areas and ate the crappy food and waited twelve hours to do nothing. I know it's not easy. I know that for every extra job you've ever done, you got up early, spent a ton of time waiting to be told what to do (maybe with a bunch of annoying people) and either never made it on set or were assigned a task and did it thirty times perfectly. And to top it off, you saw yourself when the movie came out! For this, you figure, it should go on your resume! Not so. Why? Resumes are for roles that you had to audition for, and compete with other actors to get. Credits on your resume are hard-won. They're difficult to come by, and getting them takes nerve, perseverance and time. It takes none of that to be an extra. So don't cheapen the credits you have by including extra work.

Besides blatantly making jobs up, the most dishonest thing you can do is try to pass off that kind of stuff as a real role in a production. I've seen it many times; actors who list a credit as if it were a real speaking role.

Film	Road To Perdition (thug)	dir: Sam Mendes	Dreamworks
	Public Enemies (waiter)	dir: Michael Mann	Universal
	Crooks & Liars (skater dude)	dir: D. Rector	Orion

On the surface, this actor looks like he's snagged some good roles in great movies, but if he's asked about them, he'll either have to lie, or fess up that he was an extra on all of these sets. There's a difference between being a thug as an extra and being a thug as a result of a casting process. Make sure that if you're listing film/TV work, that you had to audition for it, get called back for it, and saw your name on the call sheet (the day's shooting schedule) when it came time to work. If your name isn't on the call sheet, you're not going to be credited and it's considered extra work. Not resume worthy. This also goes for stand-in work (filling in for the main actors while the lighting is adjusted for the shot).

Background work really doesn't belong on a professional actor's resume, but if you've done a ton of it and you simply must tell the world about it, put it under the "training" category. Something like "worked as a background player in over 10 productions" should do the trick. If you do a lot of stand-in work, say "worked as 2nd team in over 15 productions."

What if you were hired as an extra for a union shoot, and they gave you a line? This is called an upgrade, and it's rare. If it happens, do a little happy dance because it means more money, possible residual income and greater recognition. It also means the job is now resume-worthy, but don't dance too long. There are different upgrade rules for different kinds of work, so it should only go on your resume if you're asked to fill out all kinds of paperwork for payroll and the union. Check with your extra coordinator or the second assistant director, to make sure you've been upgraded.

Other Things to Think About

There's another category that I don't include on my resume, but might be something you can include, and that's improvisation. Chicago is a huge center for improv training and performance, and if you're an improviser, you definitely want people to know. In terms of format, list the company and show that you did and put the best stuff first.

Sometimes actors ask if they should include any prior or current careers. I say that it depends on the job. There's a very successful actor in town who's a Chicago fireman, and that's on his resume. There are former cops who are now actors and they get lots of cop roles in films that come into town. If you've got military service in your past, or you're still serving in the reserves, put it on there. If you happen to be a doctor, nurse, or EMT, that's good for people to know, too. These are careers that perk up interest among decision makers because they have a certain cool factor associated with them. People know it's hard to be a fireman, so automatically there'll be a little built-in admiration for you. Also, the decision makers can fit you into a mold they might have in their head. If they see that you either are or were a cop, they're going to assume you'll make a terrific one as an actor. The thought is that since you did that job already in real life you'd bring a sense of authenticity to the role, which may or may not be true, but it doesn't matter. It alone might get you the audition. Also, if you've had a career that few other people have either because it's too dangerous (high-rise window washer) or it's not something you can't do in the Chicago area (lobsterman), or it's crazy difficult (brain surgeon), include it. The cooler and wackier – the better. If you don't have anything that unique in your past, don't worry about listing former careers. No one's going to care that you were an accountant for eight years, or that you worked your way through college in the pest control business. No one has anything against mundane jobs; they just won't help your acting career.

No matter how pretty your headshot is, or how compelling your resume is, neither will do you any good unless they're seen by the people doing the hiring. For that, you'll need an agent. And Chicago's got you covered.

Chicago Headshot Photographers:

I've personally used all of these shooters with great results. None of them paid me for my endorsement. Check them out online first; then, contact them for more information.

- Brian McConkey
  www.brianmcconkeyphotography.com
- Janna Giacoppo
  www.jannagiacoppo.com
- Popio Stumpf Photography
  www.popiostumpf.com

CHAPTER SIX

Agents In Chicago

U p until this point, everything we've talked about has been totally within your control. What your headshots look like, how your resume is written and how much, or little, you've trained has all been up to you. You even determine how much experience you have since there are ways of getting yourself working with whatever medium interests you. Finding an agent is also up to you, but the decision to represent you is up to them. There are ways to increase your chances of success, but first, let's talk about what an agent really does.

There are some myths out there about agents. One is that agents "discover" actors and make them famous. This is absolutely not true in Chicago. First off, agents don't actively go out looking to discover anyone. There are plenty of actors looking for representation, so the agent doesn't have to look any further than their mailbox to find new talent. That's not to say they don't approach actors once in a while. A friend of mine was doing a show and when her agent came to see it, she noticed someone in the cast that was interesting to her. After the performance the agent asked for the actor's contact information. This kind of thing isn't typical, but it does happen. Secondly, the thought of an agent discovering someone is a notion from old Hollywood carried on in modern times by entertainment networks on cable TV. Any actor who's in the public eye has gotten there through a combination of luck, talent, perseverance and timing. They were not discovered. No agent ever came up to them in a diner and exclaimed "I'm gonna make you a star!" Having an agent in your corner is invaluable, but if you ask one what their job is, none of them will tell you that it's to make their actors famous.

So what is their job? In Chicago, they're the gatekeepers of the work. Clients that need to hire actors call agents, describe what they're looking for, and the agent auditions the talent that are right for the job. Or, casting directors call agents looking for talent, and the agent sends actors to their auditions. Either way, if you want to make a living as an actor, you've got to have an agent. Once you've gotten the job, the agent negotiates your pay, coordinates the logistics of the booking, collects payment from the client when the job is done and then pays you. From the time you get the call for the audition, to the time you get your check, all the information about that job will come through your agent. *That's* their job. Not to make anyone famous, but to facilitate the work that comes across their desk.

As payment for their service, agents are entitled to a fee. Union actors pay a 10% commission on what the job pays, and nonunion actors pay 15%. This goes for everything except live work (trade shows, corporate events) and print work, which usually carry a 20% commission whether you're union or not.

While we're on the topic of agent commissions, there are a couple of things to keep in mind. Under some circumstances the client pays the agent commission, not the actor. For example, if you're a union actor and work under the AFTRA contract, the 10% agent fee will be paid by the client, not by you. So if the job pays $1000, you'll walk away with the whole amount because the $100 commission will be paid by the client. Most often, though, you should expect the agent fee to come out of your paycheck.

Also, only the fee for the job is subject to a commission. If you're paid a little extra for travel, or you're reimbursed for an expense you incurred while on the job, you won't have to pay a commission on that money.

The biggest thing for all new actors to remember is that agents can't legally charge a fee to represent you. If you ever run into an agent that asks you for money before you do any work, run far away from them. They're not legitimate. None of the agents I will refer you to will do this, but that doesn't mean that unscrupulous operations aren't out there.

Agents can, however, charge you for publicity services, like posting your headshot or voice demos on their websites. This charge might come before you do any work, which is legal. The unions set a ceiling for that cost, but there's no one setting the rates for nonunion agents. There's a growing trend of agents charging talent to have their materials on the agent's website. The thought is that if the agent is investing in a site and the talent are the ones that will gain the most from it, the agent should be allowed to recoup some of the cost. I guess I understand that, but my personal feeling is that having a company website is a cost of doing business. Many working actors have their own site anyway, which they pay for out of their own pocket. Why hit them up again? The thing is, clients are looking at your agent's website every day, so having a presence on it is important for your visibility. Whether or not you choose to pay the fees is up to you, but being on your agent's website will never hurt you. It'll only help clients find you more easily.

Another myth, or misconception about agents, is that actors work for them. Not so. Agents technically work for actors, and the good ones keep this in mind. But good actors think of it more as a partnership. A successful agent-actor relationship means that both are working toward a common goal. If the agent is doing their job, and the actor is doing what the agent suggests, the actor's career will advance and both parties win: the actor works and earns more, and the agent does too.

Because every actor in town needs an agent, competition is fierce for representation. Agents can be choosey about who they want on their roster, because there's an unlimited supply of actors and a limited supply of agents. Agents have all the work. So it's easy to forget the fact that the actor pays the agent's salary. Actors have agents for two things: their contacts and their advice. In addition to coordinating auditions and jobs, good agents also care deeply about what their talent do with their careers, and will tell you what they think if you ask them. You should take advantage of their expertise as much as possible, because most often your agent will know much more about the Chicago market than you will. But don't get cocky and take this whole "I pay your salary" attitude too far. Treat agents with respect and as knowledgeable partners in your career, not like employees.

Working With An Agent

In Chicago, there are two ways to work with agents. Actors can be exclusive or multi-listed. Both have their pros and cons. I'll discuss exclusivity first. If you're exclusive with a talent agency, then you do all of your work through that agent, and you're not represented by anyone else. All of your auditions will come through them, and even if you get a job from a source other than that agent, like if someone contacts you directly with a job, you're obligated to tell your agent and pay them a commission on those earnings.

Exclusivity gives you, the actor, the knowledge that your agent will put you on each and every audition that you're right for. As an exclusive talent, you'll have a partner in your career, someone who works on your behalf to help you make as much money as possible. When you do well, they do well, so you're always on their mind. This is what you want from an agent: to think of you as often as possible because the more you audition, the more you'll work. Sometimes agencies don't offer exclusivity to an actor unless he or she is booking a lot of work through them already.

When they realize they have a valuable actor, they understandably like to lock them up. Other agencies expect actors to be exclusive with them from the get go.

Another perk to being exclusive at an agency is that you'll get the first crack at an audition spot. If a client only wants to see five actors for a project, you can bet it'll be five exclusives instead of a combination of multi-listed actors and exclusives. This is part of the exclusivity deal: you work with that agent only and you get more chances to make money.

The downside of being exclusive is that you're passing on the chance to work with the clients of other agencies. Some clients bypass casting directors by going directly to agents to find talent, and they may be loyal to one particular agency. This is especially true of industrial and print work. The good news is that you'll be able to work for anyone that calls your agent. The bad news is that you won't have access to the producers that only work with other agencies. The way around this is to make a good decision about who to go exclusive with. You want to be with a very busy agency that has a lot of its own clients. Then it won't matter that you're missing out on opportunities that other agents have, since you'll have plenty of your own.

Agent Hopping

The other way to work with agents is to be multi-listed, which means that you can work with as many agents as will take you. Auditions will come from all of them, and none of them will have any right to claim you can't work with anyone else. You could conceivably be represented by every agent in the city. Being multi-listed means you can work with as many clients as possible, obviously a great benefit. Casting directors contact most of the talent agencies in town when they have an audition, so you're theoretically covered no matter which agent you're with (and agents with multi-listed talent assume this). You'll also have a chance to work with clients who bypass casting directors and go directly to agents. Obviously, the more agents who represent you, the more work you can potentially have.

Being multi-listed sounds like a great idea until you have too many agents and they start to conflict with each other. Sometimes multiple agents get the call to audition talent for the same job. Clients figure that if they contact more agents, they'll get to see a more diverse group of actors. The same thing happens with casting directors; they put calls out to nearly every agent in town about the same booking. If you're with three agents, and they all decide to put you on the same audition, whoever calls you first gets you, making you spoken for from that point forward. If another agent calls you for the same project, you have to tell them you're already on it. This tends to make agents unhappy. If it happens too many times, some may just stop calling because you're not available enough for them.

The other downside to being multi-listed is that there's really no one in your corner. An agent will put your name on a long list of actors who are registered with their agency, and that's the extent of your relationship until someone learns that you can book work. There's little individual attention paid to any multi-listed actor because there's simply no incentive for the agent to push any one talent unless the actor is truly right for the job. You're not guaranteed a spot in every audition you're right for. Agents sometimes figure you're covered by other talent agencies, so they don't always include you in everything.

Which Is Right For You?

When you're new in town, or new to the business, I think you should be with as many agents as possible. This gives you the best chance of meeting the most people. I was multi-listed for years, which allowed me to get to know a lot of agencies. I learned what it was like working with each one, and found that I preferred some more than others. Through the process of auditioning and working through all of them, I had good and bad experiences. I learned who paid quickly, who didn't, who fought for the actor, who fought for the client at the actor's expense and which agents seemed more interested in their bottom line than yours. It was a great education.

I could never get every agency in town interested in me, but I've worked with most of them. At one point I was represented by nine, which got to be too much. I found myself spending more time saying 'no' than 'yes'. I'd get four calls for the same audition and have to tell three agents that I couldn't work with them on it. Then there were times an agent had something for me on a day that I was already booked to work through a different agent. I'd have to tell them 'no'. This started happening a lot, and I began cutting back. I took stock of my time with each agency and made some choices. I let the good ones know that I wanted to work more with them and became deliberately less available to the ones I didn't gel with. Incidentally, two of the agencies I dropped are no longer in business.

Eventually I was down to one agent for VO and two for everything else. Of those two, I was working the most with Stewart Talent, who noticed the same thing and offered to take me on exclusively. After years of being with multiple agents, I had to think about it a little before I agreed. I always thought that if I was going to be exclusive with anyone, it would be Stewart since I had such a good relationship with everyone there. It also helped that they had a long list of clients who were loyal to them. And the clincher was that their industrial department was busier than any other agent I had ever worked with. Since industrials were my cash cow, it made sense for me to be with Stewart.

What About You?

The story of how I started as a multi-listed actor and wound up exclusive is a pretty common one. How will you know when or if it's time for you to go exclusive with an agent? It's hard to say, but there are a few things to consider. First, not all agencies work with multi-listed actors. There are those who want talent to be loyal to their office only. As you submit your materials and get responses, you'll find out which ones operate in that manner. I would tell you which ones these are, but according to actors out there working with some of these agents, this policy isn't always enforced. If an agent asks you to go exclusive with them right out of the gate before you've worked with them at all, ask for a trial period so that you can get to know them before committing. They should be fine with that, since that gives them the opportunity to get to know you, too. If they don't agree, then it's up to you to decide if you want to sign your career over to someone you don't really know. It could work out well, or it could be a bad move. I recommend getting to know as many agents as you can before putting your career in the hands of just one.

On the flip side, you'll run into agents who only work with multi-listed actors. They don't offer exclusivity to anyone. This isn't a bad thing, it's just a business decision they've made. One agent I spoke with said the agency decided not to offer exclusivity because they can't guarantee that anyone, exclusive or not, will get work. They didn't feel right about locking an actor down without that assurance. You may not know right away which agents work like this unless you ask, but typically the non-union agents skip exclusivity. The nature of being multi-listed means you may feel more like a number than a name, but that's not necessarily a bad thing. These agents still get actors lots of work. I had great relationships with offices like these for years.

Some agencies prefer to work on somewhat of a hybrid basis; that is, they don't mind if you're with other agencies but they want you to limit it to one or two rather than as many as you can find. This kind of arrangement is done on the honor system because there's no exclusive agreement signed by either party. The agent is saying they'd rather be on a short list of your agents rather than be one in a long succession. In this way, they're acknowledging the advantage and flexibility of actors having multiple agents, but they want to minimize the chance that someone else will snap you up for an audition. This is sort of a compromise on both sides and could work just fine for you. If you feel like you're being given as many chances as possible to audition and work, the number of agents you have shouldn't matter. On the other hand, if you feel like you're being held back by committing to just two agents when you could be working with more, then you should make a change.

You'll know when you're ready to be exclusive with an agent when you start to feel like you're spinning your wheels working with everyone. After you've worked for a while and developed a sense of what you want from your career, you'll start to realize who gives you the best chance of getting it and you'll want to have a deeper relationship with them. My advice is to look carefully at who you choose. If you know you're bound for TV and film work in L.A., then you know not to go with the agent who has never gotten you that kind of audition. Make sure that your agent of choice has clients besides casting directors who can offer you work. If you sign with an agent that has few opportunities outside of the ones casting directors offer, you're better off staying multi-listed.

If you agree to sign an exclusivity agreement with an agent and you're multi-listed, you'll need to let all your other agents know about your decision. How you do it depends on your relationship with the agency. Call the agents you've been frequently working with and send a letter to the ones who wouldn't recognize you if you passed them on the street. Be prepared for all of them to be unhappy. No matter how much or little you've worked with an agency, none of them likes to hear that they won't have the chance to work with you any longer. You're taking away a potential source of revenue, which is hard for any business to swallow. Simply explain that you're making a decision you feel is right for your career at this point in time.

Do you have to go exclusive? Nope. Many actors never go exclusive with an agent, so don't feel like you have to in order to make a living. If you're comfortable working with multiple agents, stick with it. As long as you're happy with the number of auditions you're getting, and you're cool with the kind of work you're being submitted for, then you're doing well. If you feel supported by your agents, and feel like you have active partners in your career development, then you really have no reason to change anything. But it's good to know that an alternative is out there.

There is a situation where you can straddle the fence between exclusivity and being multi-listed, and that's when you're exclusive with an agent for just one kind of work. I fall into this category. I do all my voice over work with Innovative Artists Chicago, and all of my on camera work with Stewart. I'm exclusive with both, but only for their respective categories. I don't do any VO through Stewart, and Innovative doesn't book me for any on camera work. In fact, occasionally the phone rings at Innovative with clients wanting to hire me for an on camera job, and the callers are told to contact Stewart. The same thing happens the other way around. This arrangement works really well for me, and it seems to work for both agents, too. Again, if it ain't broke...

Getting An Agent

One of the great things about Chicago is that our community of talent agencies is pretty diverse. There are large agencies with many agents representing hundreds of actors, and one-agent offices working with a small, core group. There are agencies that focus on working with minority actors, others that do only union work, and some only go after nonunion jobs. There are agents that only do VO, some who only do print and some that are full-service, meaning they work on anything and everything.

Whichever agent you're interested in, the process for getting represented in Chicago is pretty simple. For on camera actors, here it is, step by step:

1. Mail your fantastic headshot and brilliant resume to the agent along with a cover letter. Use a large manila envelope so your headshot doesn't have to be folded. If you've got examples of your work on DVD, include that as well. The cover letter should be short and to the point. Something like this:

Dear Molly,

I'm looking to expand my employment potential in the Chicago market and am submitting my headshot and resume for consideration by your agency. I'd love to meet with you and talk about how we could begin a mutually beneficial relationship. If you think there's a place for me in your talent pool, I can be reached either by email or by phone. Have a great day!

Sincerely,

Chris Agos
chris@actinginchicago.com
312-555-1212

2. Wait a month. This is the hardest part because you don't know what's going on and you're anxious. The agent could have looked at your stuff and decided you weren't right for their agency, or it could be sitting on their desk, or in their mail room. If you haven't heard anything from them after a month, send everything again, this time with a cover letter that reads like this:

Dear Molly,

About a month ago, I sent you a headshot and resume for consideration by Molly's Talent, Inc. As of this writing, I'm still interested in pursuing a mutually beneficial relationship with the agency, and would love to come in to read for you. If you're interested, feel free to get in touch. My contact information is below. Have a great day!

Sincerely,

Chris Agos
chris@actinginchicago.com
312-555-1212

This follow up letter is a little different than the first one, but still hits the same key points, which is that you're interested in representation, and you understand that there's got to be something in it for both parties.

3. Wait some more. Send another headshot and letter every month for six months, keeping your overall tone positive and upbeat, even if it's your sixth letter and you're ticked off beyond belief that no one's gotten in touch with you. If after six months you get no reply, give up on that agent. For now, they can't use you. But you never know, you may get a call down the road.

If you're looking for a voice over agent, the process is the same except you should mail your voice demo instead of a headshot. Don't worry about a resume, but do include a cover letter much like the examples above. If you're tempted to email your demo, don't. Large files clog agents' in-boxes and make it more difficult to conduct regular business. Mail it the old fashioned way.

Some agents have very little time during an average workday to look at all the mail they get. So they set it all aside and go through the new submissions every so often. Some do this twice a year, some maybe every quarter. That means you should expect some time to pass between when you send your materials and when you get a reply. You never know when they're going to go through the stacks. You might mail your stuff in for six months, give up on them and be pleasantly surprised by a phone call nine months after your first mailing. If you follow this system, they'll have six chances over the course of half a year to see your name. This is great because if your name sounds familiar to them, someone will eventually pick up your resume and have a look.

Most agents that represent actors for on camera work also do print, so if you're interested in doing that kind of work explore that with them after the agent expresses an interest in you. If you've already done some print work and have a comp card (a collection of looks you can pull off successfully), send it along with your headshot to show them you're capable of working print in addition to on camera. If you're looking to do trade show work, the process is much the same. Send a headshot and resume along with any footage you may have of past work you've done.

Did you notice that the process I outlined did not include calling or walking into agents' offices? Agents don't like it when actors do either. Remember, when agents are at their office they're working. They have things on their mind, phone calls to make, auditions to put together, fires to put out and money to make. They really don't have time to talk with someone they have never met before. They make time to go through all the headshots they get from actors they don't know. Calling them or walking in to their offices will not further your case. Allow time for your headshot to go through their internal process for selecting new talent.

Stick with the monthly submissions. If you feel like you just have to do more, you can send a post card here and there, especially if you're doing a show. You want to be persistent, but not annoying. It's a fine line. If you cross it by calling or walking in, you might ruin your chances of getting the agent.

They Called! Now What?

Each agency handles actors who are new to their agency in a different way. Some take the time to get to know the actor before they sign you, some don't. When I was looking for representation, I ran into two kinds of situations: agents who want you to register with them, and ones who want to meet you and see what you've got. If you're told to come in and register, your name will go on a long list of talent the agent represents. They'll ask you to stop by to fill out some forms, give them a stack of headshots or some VO demos and meet a few people at the agency. Some agents do all of this online or through the mail, which means you may never meet anyone at the agency.

The ones who want to get to know you are more interesting. You'll get a phone call or an email inviting you to their office for an audition. If it's an on camera agent, they may ask you to prepare a monologue, and will likely have a few scripts for you to read cold when you get there. Your audition might be put on tape. If it's a VO agent, they'll have copy for you to work on and read in their recording booth. Be ready for anything, and just try to relax and be yourself. Easier said than done, I know, but no one can sell you better than you. Have fun with it.

After your audition, the tape may be reviewed by the agents in the office and if there's a consensus reached in your favor, you'll be offered a spot on their roster. It may be a probationary position for a short period of time. They'll send you out on auditions and get feedback on how you do before they ask you to stay with them for the long term. You should always do your best at every audition, but this is the time to really nail each one. You want word to get back to your new agent that you do a great job, whether or not you land the job. Do well and the agent will take notice. This is exactly the kind of situation that's going to help you make a living as an actor.

My very first agent, a very nice lady who ran a one-woman agency, asked me to come in and meet her. I remember this vividly because I thought I left my house with plenty of time to get to the appointment. I didn't. I hit traffic on the expressway, missed an exit, and generally freaked out most of the way there. I even turned around illegally using one of those openings in the median for emergency vehicles. For all of my panic, the appointment went really well. I had approached her to rep me for VO. She didn't have a recording booth, so I didn't read any copy for her. We just talked about my demo, and about what kind of work I might be right for. She also suggested that I get a set of headshots. By the end of the appointment, I knew a little about her, and she knew a little about me. I was ecstatic, because now I had an agent! The phone would start ringing with auditions and I'd be making money in no time!

My second agent sent me a postcard that thanked me for my submission and asked me to drop by the office to register. It told me what to bring, and which days of the week they saw new talent. I followed the instructions to the letter, and when I showed up, I was given a clipboard with some forms to fill out. After completing them I handed them back to the receptionist along with a stack of my headshots, and I left. I was so excited! I had another agent! The phone would really be ringing now! I had double the agents, double the auditions, double the work!

There's a phenomenon that occurs when actors register with an agent, and it's called waiting. I waited a few weeks for my first phone call. That turned into a month. Then two months. Then three, four and five. I was unraveling with frustration the whole time. Here I was, trained, ready and willing to go on any and all auditions either agent had for me. I was also still submitting my demo to other agents, hoping to pick up a third. Once in a while I called to check in with both agents, who kindly informed me that they had nothing for me. Finally after nearly six months, my first agent called with an audition. I booked the job. The moral of the story is, stick with it and eventually your phone will ring.

What If They Don't Call?

No matter what agency you're submitting to, there's one universal truth about all of them: they're in business to make money. In order for them to make as much as possible, they need to have actors that are going to give them the best shot of booking work. Keep in mind that when an actor goes on an audition, they're auditioning against other actors who are represented by other talent agents. So not only is that actor competing for the job, but the agent is too. As a result, agents assemble a group of actors they think gives them the best shot at booking the highest number of jobs.

Sometimes, the agent is happy with the group they have and doesn't feel the need to add any new actors. But the group is constantly changing. People move, or switch agents, or otherwise become unavailable. When there's a hole in the talent pool, agents are more open to meeting new actors, but only ones that can plug the hole.

Let's say an agency works with about two hundred actors. The group is evenly split between men and women, and there's a good age range within each of those from young to old. But lately there's been a lot of actresses in their thirties having babies, which takes them out of the loop for a while. Suddenly, instead of having plenty of women in that age range, the agency has a shortage. They need to find actresses they don't know to take the place of the new Moms, otherwise the agency will have fewer women auditioning, which means fewer chances to make money. The agents turn to the submissions they regularly get, but they look only for women in their thirties. They don't need anyone else at the moment. If you don't fit that profile, you won't be contacted.

This is good to know because so many actors take it personally when an agent doesn't call them. Actors feel like there's something wrong with them, or they're not good enough somehow. The fact is that agents usually choose who to represent based on who is already on their roster. So if an agent passes you over, that may not say anything about your headshots, your ability, look or talent. It might just mean that they're filled up with people in your age range that would go after the same kind of work you would do and have no need to add any more. In our example, once the agency finds a bunch of actresses that can fill their gap, they call them in to read one by one. After considering all of them, the ones that stand out get the call to join the agency.

If you know you're doing everything you should be doing, boning up on your skills, doing a show now and then, keeping your look appropriate for the kind of work you're going after, then don't take the fact that an agent isn't snapping you up too seriously. Not all agents are always looking to add new people, nor are they always looking for your type.

Other Ways To Get Agents

Since we know that you need an agent, is there a trick to getting one? People find all kinds ways of getting representation. Rule number one is to be persistent. I sent my voice demo to Innovative regularly for four years before they invited me in to read for them. Their office is run by a bunch of very smart and talented ladies, and when I met one of them for the first time, she said to me "Oh, you're the guy who keeps sending me demos. You don't give up, do you?" I smiled and proceeded to read the heck out of whatever copy she put in front of me.

I only got the appointment because I was in a class with a guy who was represented by them, and he mentioned me to them after we became friends. That's one of the ways people land at talent agencies. The more people you know, the more likely you are to click with someone who's going to stick their neck out for you. I got started with Stewart in the same way. A teacher of mine thought I would fit in well there, so she mentioned my name and sparked a little interest. I can almost attribute my entire career to meeting those two people when I did. Now, this only works if the person who recommends you is a trusted and experienced actor at the agency. Agents listen to actors who are credible.

What happened to me isn't unusual. Freddie Sulit, an actor, improvisor and ear prompter specialist who does a lot of industrials and trade shows, tells a similar story. When he was working his very first trade show, he made friends with the other actors on the job. One of them thought enough of his work to recommend Freddie to his agent, which wasn't the same agent that Freddie was working with on that job. That lead to an audition for his buddy's agent, who thought Freddie was great. Freddie started landing a lot of work through his new agent. Oddly enough, his original agent never called him again after he booked that first job, but it wasn't a tragedy. His new agent made up for it. Freddie sums up his experience this way: "It pays to be friendly with other talent on a gig."

Another way to get signed by an agent is to already have a career. If you're thinking of moving to Chicago from another market and you've been in the business for a while, you'll have a very good chance of landing at an agency that will take good care of you. Agents like to work with actors who need little or no training. It's a no-brainer for them. If they spend less time showing you the ropes, they can spend more time trying to get you work. Experienced union actors should look hard at Stewart Talent, Grossman & Jack Talent and Big Mouth Talent. Experienced nonunion actors should also consider those three if they're willing to join the unions. But if you'd like to remain nonunion, look at Talent Group and Karen Stavins Enterprises.

Keep In Touch

After you've been signed up by an agent, whether it's your first or fifth, you should do everything you can to make it easy for that agent to think of you when they have something for your type. You'll want to keep in touch with the agent, but you don't want to be annoying either. In the past, actors did this thing called "making rounds." For all I know they might still do it in New York, which is where I first heard of it. That's where an actor physically stops by the agent's office just to say 'hi' and see what's going on. I'm not a big fan of this and neither are most agents in Chicago. You're not fooling anybody. They know what you're doing. You walk into their office and say "Hey, how are you today?" But if there was a cartoon thought bubble floating above your head, it would read, "PLEASE PLEASE PLEASE give me an audition today! I haven't had one in two weeks! C'mon! Whaddya got for me?" They don't have anything for you. If they did, you would have gotten a call. Yet part of your job is to stay on their mind, so you have to do something.

No actor I know randomly stops in to see his or her agent without a reason. They find reasons, ones that are legitimate so they're not standing there blatantly asking if there are any auditions. One reason that's always legit is to see if they're low on your headshots. Agents can go through them fairly quickly, so it's possible they actually might need some. If you call to ask that question, you accomplish both the job of staying on their mind and finding out if they really do need shots. But here's a caveat: a lot of agents submit actors for work electronically, which limits the number of shots they hand out. This is only getting more common, so the whole, "Hey, how you guys doing on headshots?" ruse might not last too much longer.

Another reason to stay in touch is if you're doing a show. Drop off a postcard, call to invite them, e-mail them a flyer, whatever. It's good for them to see that you're staying active. If you land a film or TV job and you're multi-listed, send a note to all the agents that didn't get you the job. Tell them where they can see you and when to watch.

When I was working hard to make an impression on new agents, I used to call and double check the details on all my jobs before I went on them. This showed that I was a careful actor who wanted to make sure I didn't make a mistake, and it gave me a great reason to call and chat with the agent. The idea is to stay in touch without looking like you're desperate to, even though you might be.

Each agent has a different policy on when, how and how often talent can check in with them. There are agents that have an open door policy. Actors can call any time and drop by as much as they want. There are also agents with a very different way of working. They don't want you to call, email, stop by or even sneeze in their direction. These kinds of agents epitomize the old phrase "Don't call us, we'll call you." When you sign up with any talent agency, ask what their check-in policy is so you don't wear out your welcome before your first audition.

Act Like You've Been There Before

While you're working with your new agent, the number one thing to remember is this – be professional. You're in the business world, even though it's a creative business. Use common sense and put your best effort forward all the time, not just in the audition room. Part of being professional means being easy to reach. In the old days agents reached me by pager. When times changed and that made me look too much like a drug dealer, I switched to a cell phone. To this day, I'm always reachable on my cell. My agents know to try that number first, but they also have my email address and other numbers. When you miss a call, return it quickly. A good way to tick off an agent is by being slow about getting back to them. Sometimes auditions come with very little notice, so you never know if that voice mail says that you need to be downtown in a hurry. Don't assume agents can wait for you to call them back. Assume they needed you yesterday.

Being professional also means showing up where you're supposed to be and on time. If you drive, parking in the city can be a real pain, so leave for your appointments with extra time. The CTA is great, except when it's late, so budget a good amount of time if you're taking public transportation. If you're going to be late to an audition because of traffic or some other unforeseen circumstance, call your agent and let them know when you'll be there. Call your agent first, no matter where the audition is located. If it's at a client's office, an ad agency, a photographer's studio or a casting director's office, your agent should be notified so that they can call the location and let them know. If you're really late, it's possible you might not be able to get in, and you don't want to show up and be turned away. Let your agent find out for you. If you're going to be late for a job, again, call the agent who booked you. When you're on the set be cordial and focused, getting the job done in a way that will make the client call your agent and compliment your work. That's how you'll get more auditions and more jobs.

After the booking, some agents like you to check in with them. They're interested in knowing how it went, but they also want to know how many hours you worked in case you went into overtime. Overtime usually means more pay, so they use your word of what happened on the set as the basis for billing the extra time. If you're a union actor, keep track of how long your lunch break was, and how many of your wardrobe choices the client used if they asked you to bring any, since there are fees associated with that. These are all things that may determine the final amount you earn for the job. If you drove to the booking and it was outside of the Chicagoland area, tell your agent your travel times and how many miles you drove. Don't wait for days to do this, get all the pertinent information to your agent no later than the day after you finish the job. This is one of those ways to stay in touch for legitimate reasons, so take advantage. Some agents don't require this, so if you're not sure, just ask what they prefer.

More than anything, being a professional actor means that you are available to work and audition. By declaring to the world that you deserve to be paid for your services, you simply must be physically available to do the things actors have to do. Nothing is more frustrating to an agent, and nothing will end the relationship faster than if you're habitually not available to do your job. Everything on this side of the acting world happens during regular business hours, so that means your auditions and jobs will happen from 9 to 5, Monday through Friday. If you have a full-time job, hopefully it's flexible enough that you can skip out when necessary. If it's not, what are you going to do? Figure out a way to work from home. Telecommute. Job share. Get a different full-time gig at night until your acting can pay your bills. Whatever. Just be available during regular business hours, or your career will be over before it starts. Chapter 12 is all about other jobs you can have while you're waiting for your acting career to develop.

When you know you're not going to be available to audition or work, call your agent and tell them. This is called "booking yourself out". You book out when you're going to be on vacation, going to work another job or taking a class that meets during the day. Some agents want you to book out for everything, even auditions. Others just want to know when you're going to be out of town. Check with the agencies you're with to find out their preferences.

Once you've done the job, it's okay to ask your agent how long they think it might take for you to get paid for the job. If the agent has a history with the client, they may be able to tell you whether the client pays quickly or not. This information will help when it's been a while and you're wondering where your money is. If you're a union actor, there are safeguards in place that pretty much assure you'll have a check within a month or so; although that's not to say it can't take longer. If you're non-union, it could take quite a bit longer, up to 120 days. If you think about it, the money's got to go through several entities before it winds up in your hands. The company you worked for has to be paid by their client, which might have to get a check from somewhere else. Once your agent gets a check, they'll cut you one.

Head Games

In times when business is booming and you feel like you're in a groove, you'll love your agent(s). You'll feel like you're a valuable cog in a well-oiled machine. When times are slow and you're sitting at home wondering where all the auditions are, you'll feel like the machine has rusted to a halt and you won't know why. It's easy to blame them. You think they're not sending you out, they're deliberately hiding work from you, or that they just don't like you anymore. I used to page myself just to make sure my pager was actually working.

Actors are good at assuming things, and I think that comes from having no insight into what goes on in your agent's office from day to day. Agents don't disclose information about what their actors are working on because that information is between the agent and the talent. It's not for public consumption. So you'll have no idea what other actors are doing. It might be nothing, or it might be tons of work. No one but the agents actually know if their phones are ringing, or if clients are calling for actors who are your type, or if the casting directors have anything in the works. We just assume their phone is ringing off the hook, projects are falling into their laps left and right and everyone else is auditioning and working, so we should be too. We have to think like that to help us deal with the uncertainty of being a freelancer. We have to believe there's enough work out there for everyone, because if there isn't, how the heck will there ever be enough to allow us to get our share? How will we make the mortgage payment?

While it's true that there is some kind of job happening every single day in this market, there are times when it's just really slow. That has nothing to do with you, nor does it have anything to do with your agent or your agent's view of you. It simply means that they don't have anything for you at the moment. The only predictable thing about this business is that it's unpredictable.

Do agents drop talent? Yes. But when that happens, it's for a reason. You'll be notified when it does and you'll be told why. But if you don't get a call letting you know that they won't be working with you anymore, just assume that there's simply nothing available for you at the moment. Check in as often as they've welcomed you to, and stay positive that something will happen for you sooner or later.

The Party's Over

Is there ever a time for an actor to break up with an agent instead of the other way around? Sure. Remember Freddie Sulit? He didn't need the agent that landed him his first trade show. After that one job, they never called him again. But it didn't matter because he had plenty of work from the agent he met by doing that job. If you're multi-listed, and you've got an agent or two that you never hear from, why waste time and headshots on them? You don't want to hit the break-up button too quickly, but if you've been holding up your end of the deal by keeping in touch, following their policies, and staying available for anything that might come up, you should eventually get some positive reinforcement. If you don't, do you really want to be with that agent?

When I was nonunion, one of the agents I worked with was Karen Stavins Enterprises. It took me some time to get in with them, and once I did, they were a tough nut to crack. I knew they had a lot of work, but I wasn't getting calls from them. One day I was doing some extra work on a commercial in Wisconsin. I was part of a crowd scene and a nice lady was positioned next to me. Since there were long stretches of time where we had nothing to do, we started chatting. I found out that she worked part-time at Stavins. I mentioned that I was with them, and she looked at me funny. She said, "Really?" Terrific. Someone who worked there just confirmed that I wasn't in their loop at all. I nodded and told her I hadn't been contacted for anything since registering. Aloud, she wondered why. I just kept shrugging because I didn't have a clue. By the time this exchange happened, she had worked with me the whole day and knew I was good on a set, good with following directions and a nice person. That was all she needed. "Do you have any headshots on you?" I did, and gave her a couple. She eyeballed my resume, and explained to me why I may not have been called yet. "You're pretty young, and a lot of what we get goes to older guys. Also, it can just be hard for new people to break through. The agents have their list of people they know they can count on, so they usually just call in the same actors, especially if there are only a few spots available. Why risk a job on someone new who might stink? If an actor does a bad audition, the agent just looks like they don't know how to do their job." She looked at me for a second as I nodded along with her reasoning. Finally she said, "I'll see what I can do," as she stashed my headshots in her bag. The next week, I had an audition at Stavins. And not long after that, I booked a large client that brought a lot of work to the agency. From that point on, I was on their short list. I don't know who I bumped off of it, but I'm glad there was room for me.

I've said that perseverance is the key to being successful in this business. But there's also a time for a reality check. If you've got an agent who simply won't allow you to play the game, you have the right to walk off the field. How long you wait before you do that is up to you, but I'd say that 18 months is a good timeframe. It can take that long for you to break into their system. If it's been a one-sided relationship that whole time, I think you've got to be realistic and call it quits with that agent. You'll have enough uncertainty in this business, and you don't need it from someone who's supposed to be supportive.

There are other reasons to break up with an agent. One actor told me about an agent who used his computer skills more than his acting skills. The agency would call him when their Internet was down, or when they were having issues with their website, but they wouldn't call him to audition for anything. After a while they started giving his name out to actors who needed their reels edited. That was the last nail in the coffin. He dumped them, and rightly so.

If you have problems getting paid from your agent, you should make a change. Good agents know that they didn't earn that money, you did, and it belongs to you, not them. It's reasonable that they won't pay you until they get paid, but if you consistently have to wait five, six, seven months (or more!) to get a check for your work, why would you continue to give them interest-free loans? You're an actor, not a bank. Dump them.

Most agents are terrific. All the agents I'll mention treat their actors with great respect. They are very responsible with every aspect of the business they run. They work hard for the actors they represent, and are very good at what they do. Keeping tabs on the relationship you have with your agent is just another part of your job as an actor, because things don't always go the way you think they should.

Speaking of things not going according to plan, after a quick review of some of Chicago's agents, let's talk about auditions next.

Chicago Talent Agencies

I've either worked with these agencies personally, or have friends who are represented by them. None of them paid me for my endorsement. Agents not included in this list may be great. Don't assume that agencies I don't mention aren't worth checking out.

Stewart Talent

If you've done any asking around about agents in Chicago, you've heard of Stewart Talent. It's one of the busiest talent agencies in the city, and also has offices in New York and Atlanta. Stewart has departments representing actors for work in all seven areas of the business and even has a department devoted to child actors and print models. They also have a very busy fashion model division.

Stewart has strong relationships with producers, ad agencies and photographers. Clients often call the agents at Stewart directly for talent. For actors, that means you're competing only with other people in the agency instead of with everyone in the city. If you're looking to become a career actor, it'll be hugely beneficial to be with an agency that has its own clients.

Turnover is very low at Stewart, both among the agents and the actors. It's rare to hear of an actor leaving the agency, and even rarer to hear of an agent leave. Because of this, Stewart can be difficult for an actor to break into. As the big kid on the block, agents there are inundated with actor submissions and can afford to be very selective. That doesn't mean it's impossible to get them interested in you, but you do have to be persistent.

Stewart is a good place for seasoned performers to consider. Actors who have some good resume credits are more likely to get a look than those just beginning their career. That doesn't mean you shouldn't submit if you're new. Remember, you may fill a hole in their talent pool. Stewart mostly books union work but also works with nonunion performers on a limited basis.

Stewart Talent
58 W Huron St
Chicago, IL 60654
www.stewarttalent.com

Big Mouth Talent

A lot of talent agencies spring from older, more established ones. Back in the day I walked into an agent's office and had a brief chat with a receptionist named Brooke. Jump ahead about five years, and I heard there's a new boutique agency working with a small group of actors. That sounded interesting, so I submitted to Big Mouth Talent. When I read for them, I ran into Brooke again, who this time was the owner. I worked with her for a while and had a great experience.

Today the agency is run by Kelly McLaughlin. The agency represents a little more than a hundred actors. Keeping the group small allows Kelly to get to know all of them more personally than she would if there were hundreds of actors to track. For actors, this means there's no wondering if you're getting the attention you need. You can bet if you're one of Big Mouth's actors, you're being submitted for everything you should be.

Whether union or not, Big Mouth only works with actors on an exclusive basis. The agency is very loyal to their talent and wants the same commitment in return.

Actors who want to submit to Big Mouth should mail in a headshot, resume and reel, if they have one. Skip the email, stick with snail mail. And if you're a voice talent, you're out of luck because Big Mouth doesn't do VO.

Big Mouth Talent
900 N Franklin St # 709
Chicago, IL 60610
www.bigmouthtalent.com

Grossman & Jack

Grossman & Jack also ranks high on the list of agents with which actors want to work. The agency has been around for about 30 years, and represents actors for on camera, VO and print. They've recently added Agency Galatea, a division representing fashion models.

When you're hunting for an agency, you want to stick with ones that have a good reputation around town, and Grossman & Jack is on that list. Like Stewart, actors tend to stay with them for a long time.

Submit to Grossman & Jack like you would any agency. They do lots of union work, but also will work with nonunion actors who are interested in making the jump.

Grossman & Jack Talent
33 W Grand Avenue, Suite 402
Chicago, IL 60654
www.grossmanjack.com

Innovative Artists Chicago

Innovative is known primarily for representing voice talent, but also works with a limited number of on camera actors. The company traces its roots back to the 1980's when Sharon Wottrich, an agent at a full-service agency, opened Voices Unlimited. VU was devoted strictly to representing voice talent. This was a risky move at the time since no one had ever tried a niche agency in Chicago. The decision paid off, and today the agency is nationally known for representing Grade-A voice talent. In 2006, Voices Unlimited became the Chicago office of Los Angeles-based Innovative Artists.

I've been with the agency since 2000 and can vouch for the high quality of the agents there. An interesting thing about being an Innovative talent is that the L.A. and New York offices are open to us when we're in those cities. Occasionally I find myself in L.A., and I'm able to grab an audition when I'm there. Chicago-based talent are also frequently put on auditions coming out of the L.A. or NYC offices.

If you're a voice talent interested in getting represented at Innovative, mail a demo to their address. Don't email a file. The agents prefer voice talent who come from an acting background, but if your demo stands out in some way, and they happen to be looking for your voice type, you may get a call for an audition. On camera actors should mail a headshot and resume. Be prepared to join the unions if you aren't a member because Innovative only books union work. They're open to working with nonunion performers who want to join SAG and AFTRA.

Innovative Artists Chicago
541 N Fairbanks Ct, Ste. 2735
Chicago, IL 60611
www.iachicago.com

Karen Stavins Enterprises & Corporate Presenters

Karen Stavins Enterprises is Chicago's oldest talent agency devoted strictly to doing nonunion work. They're very professional and look after their actors with care. When I was working with them, Karen once said to me, "It's not my money, it's yours." If you're looking for proof that they're good people to work with, that's it. The agency represents adult actors for all areas of the business.

Stavins works with multi-listed talent and does not offer exclusivity. Actors are free to work with other agents if they feel it will benefit their career. Check their website for submission guidelines.

Karen Stavins Enterprises & Corporate Presenters
303 E. Wacker Dr., Concourse Level
Chicago, IL 60601
www.karenstavins.com

Talent Group

Another agency devoted to representing nonunion actors, Talent Group has been around since 1987. They represent about 350 adult actors for commercials, voice over, industrials and print. They've got a good reputation among actors around town, and when they represented me, they always played by the rules.

Submit to Talent Group by mailing in your materials following the schedule outlined in this chapter.

Talent Group, Inc.
4755 N Hermitage Ave
Chicago, IL 60640
www.mytalentgroup.com

Trade Show Agencies

While Stewart and Karen Stavins represent actors for the trade show industry, there isn't an agency in Chicago devoted strictly to that line of work. But if you're really interested in getting a lot of trade show work, you might consider looking to agents located in other cities. I haven't worked with any of these agencies, but they come highly recommended from other actors I know. Check out Patrick Talent, Productions Plus and the Renee Godin Agency. Google them for their websites and submission policies.

CHAPTER SEVEN

Auditioning in Chicago

Imagine getting together with fifty, sixty, or a hundred of your closest friends, all of you united for one common purpose. That's one way to look at an audition. Some think of it as a game, others see it as a firing squad. However you look at it, you might as well get comfortable with auditions. They're a hurdle all actors have to conquer to reach their goals, dreams and paychecks. But they don't have to be adversarial. They are there to help you.

No matter how successful you become in Chicago, you'll always have to audition for work. You might audition less as your past clients begin to book you without one, but for all new opportunities, you're going to have to give decision makers a chance to see if you're right for the job.

If you're freaked out about auditioning, it's easy to see why. The high stakes make it nerve-wracking. I can give you all kinds of tips and tricks to help you with your mindset, but they're just different ways of telling you the same thing: you need to get over it. As a professional actor, you have to bring your A-game to every audition, no matter what. That ability comes from experience, which we'll talk about in this chapter.

If you're past the point where you're queasy about auditioning, I hope you've kept a good attitude about the process. Your time in this business will go much easier than those who perceive it as a nuisance. I've heard plenty of actors in waiting rooms say something like, "This is so stupid, why can't they just cast us off our headshots?" I've even felt like that sometimes, but that kind of mindset works against what you're there for in the first place: a chance to earn money doing what you love. A bad attitude is a good way to become a professional auditioner instead of a working actor.

Another reason to stay positive about auditions is that you never know who is going to see your work. In Chicago, many directors pursue multiple types of work. You might be auditioning for a commercial, but the director also happens to be looking for someone for his first film. You may not be right for the spot, but you might be perfect in his movie. Remember my initial experience with Karen Stavins Enterprises? I had a tough time getting noticed until I met someone who opened the door for me. One of the first auditions I did there was for a department store in Nebraska. I didn't get the job, but the ad agency thought I might be good for one of their other clients. They asked me to do another audition, this time for a local cellular phone company, and I got the job. The phone people kept me as their spokesperson for a long time. I did all their TV and radio spots, along with some print. When you're auditioning for one project, you're actually auditioning for everything else the decision makers are working on at the time. So keep your head up.

Auditions are a necessary part of the profession. Both actors and the clients who hire them have wondered if there's a better way of choosing talent for a job, but the trusty audition has been the only thing that stuck through the years. Though we're not paid for them (usually), most actors view auditions as part of their job. After all, there's no paying work without auditions. Since they're so important, it's good to know what to expect.

The Process

Seasoned actors will find no surprises when they audition in Chicago. Auditions here work just like those in L.A., Austin or New York. Arranged by casting directors or agents, watched over by cameras, clients and microphones, it's a chance for the decision makers to compare actors and choose their cast. The setup should be familiar, only the setting will have changed. Regardless of where it takes place, scripts are almost always provided ahead of time unless it's a VO audition where you may be expected to read the copy with little time to look at it. In either case you'll do your audition piece once as you've prepared it. The person running the audition might ask you to try a couple of tweaks, and you'll do it again. Once everyone's happy, you're done.

If you're new to auditioning in a professional environment, let's start at the beginning. Your phone will ring, and it'll be your agent. You'll be told what the project is, what kind of role you're auditioning for and given an appointment time and location. You might also be given callback and shoot dates, which you should check against your calendar to make sure you're available. If you're not free on those dates, tell your agent. He or she will either tell you to skip it or go anyway to see what happens. If you go, tell who ever is auditioning you that you have a schedule conflict.

Let's assume you're available. Most likely you'll be emailed a script. On rare occasions the scripts aren't ready until the day of the audition, so you'll get them when you show up for the audition. This usually only happens if the role you're auditioning for has very few lines. Most agents and casting directors try hard to get actors their scripts with plenty of time to prepare.

The one time you may not get a script is when you're auditioning for a role that has no lines at all. These are called MOS auditions. Your agent will say something like, "This audition is MOS." MOS is an acronym that stands for "Mitt Out Sound," and no, that's not a typo. There's a bit of legend that explains why we call them MOS auditions, and it goes way back. The story goes like this: In the 1930's there was a German film director working in Hollywood. One day he arrived on the set of his latest movie to find the day's shot being set up. He noticed that the audio crew was placing microphones around the set, and he stopped them. Yelling at them in loud, heavily accented English, he said, "Nein! Dees eez mit out sound!" He was trying to say "No! This is without sound!" But his accent made "with" come out as "mitt". It stuck and morphed into an acronym. To this day, everyone in the business calls a scene without lines MOS. Each letter is pronounced separately, like when you're talking about IBM, the huge technology company. They're not called moss scenes. I have no idea if this story is true or not, but it's told over and over, so I assume it's at least partly based in fact.

Once you have all of the information your agent has, you should spend some time with however many scripts you're sent. The tough auditions are the ones where you're sent a lot of material, and you're told to be familiar with all of it. That doesn't mean you need to memorize everything, but you should be able to do them while not having your head buried in the script. I was once sent eight scripts to look at for an audition. Eight! Can you believe that? It was for a series of commercials, and I was auditioning for the one role that showed up in every spot. Whoever got cast was going to have a ton of work, but it was a job and a half just preparing for it. I was told to be ready to do any of them. I had a day or two to get to know my way around all the scenes, so I spent a good amount of time with each one. By the time I walked into the audition room, I could do almost all of them from memory. I felt great about it. When I got to the casting office, they told everyone in the waiting room that we'd only do two of them. I was so bummed. After working that hard on eight scripts, I wanted to do them all. But this just goes to show that no matter how much material you're given, they really only have a certain amount of time to get all the actors on tape. These were all :30 second spots, so if we did them back-to-back without stopping in between, it would have taken four minutes. With setup time for each one and multiple takes, each actor would have been in front of a camera for at least ten minutes. That's an eternity in the audition room. Usually you're in and out much faster than that. Still, you never know what you're going to walk into, so if you've been given eight scripts, be ready to do them all.

Wardrobe

You should give some thought to what you're going to wear to the audition. In the on camera world it's called your wardrobe, not your costume, which is the term used when you're working on stage. Sometimes you'll be told exactly what they want to see. Other times, it'll be up to you. If you're left to figure it out on your own, look to the script for clues. If you're reading for the part of a doctor, you'll probably need a lab coat or scrubs if the scene is set in a hospital. If the scene takes place between two actors just getting out of bed, you'll want to audition in your PJs. I once auditioned for a bank commercial, yet the role I was up for was that of a jogger. I showed up wearing my running clothes.

If you're not specifically told what to wear, there are three styles, or looks that are often used as a general guideline:

1. Professional – this means suits and ties for men, and suits or jacket/skirt outfits for women. Think two lawyers arguing in a courtroom, a couple of bankers sealing a deal, or a high-powered boardroom meeting.
2. Business casual/nice casual – khakis and button down shirts for men and khakis or more casual skirts and nice tops for women. Think a nice night out on the weekend, or working in an office with a less formal dress code. Sometimes you can get away with

jeans, but only if they look like they could be pants and don't have any rips, tears or distressed style to them.

3. Casual – whatever you'd wear around the house. Jeans and polos for the guys, jeans and casual tops for the women. Think running errands on a Saturday afternoon or watching the big game with friends. Don't go too sloppy here. Make sure you're not wearing your grubbiest shirt unless you're asked to bring it.

Whatever you wear, you'll need to follow a couple rules. First and foremost, make sure it's appropriate for the role. Follow the directions you're given, and if you're not given any, read the script and give it your best guess. Look to TV shows or commercials that have the same kind of setup as the one you're auditioning for and use what the actors are wearing as a starting point. Unless you're told otherwise, your wardrobe choice should be three things: in step with current style (don't dress like you're paying homage to the 80's), age appropriate (moms should leave their teens' clothes at home), and modest. Ladies, skip the top with the plunging neckline and the super short skirt unless you're told to wear the sexiest thing you have.

Secondly, stay away from anything that's striped. Cameras don't deal with stripes on clothing very well. The reason is a bit technical, but it comes down to how the chips and sensors in the camera process information. Stripes can sometimes produce an effect called a moiré pattern, which are ripples or waves moving on the screen over the striped piece of clothing. This is distracting and you want the decision makers to watch you, not your striped tie.

Thirdly, most video cameras don't like white clothing. The camera can't decide whether the focal point of the shot is the bright color of the garment or the darker tone of your skin, resulting in the camera's iris constantly adjusting to compensate. Same goes for black clothing. Earth tones, warm colors and soft pastels do really well on camera. Grays and jewel tones are nice, too. Red sometimes makes some skin tones look funny, so most actors skip it and go for more subdued colors.

Also, unless the audition calls for a sloppy look, don't show up looking like you just slept overnight in a car. Iron, steam or press your clothes. And you might want to press both the front *and* back of your shirt - just a suggestion.

Lastly, don't forget about your feet. This is more for the guys, I think. You never know how wide they're going to shoot you. Don't assume that the client will never see your shoes. If you're auditioning in the middle of January and there's a foot of snow on the ground, don't wear your boots in the room with your suit. If you're dressed well, bring a good pair of shoes. I see this all the time, people (men and women) who look good from their ankles up, but forget that their shoes are part of their look, too. After a while all of this will become second nature to you.

Be A Pro

On the audition day, get there on time. Being late may cost you the chance to audition. I try to make it to every audition fifteen minutes early so I can find parking, check in and read any additional information that might be posted before my actual time slot. If you're auditioning at a casting director's office, usually there's a short questionnaire for you to fill out called an information sheet. Casting directors use these to get your clothing sizes and conflicts for the job dates. Don't lie about your sizes or measurements, and make sure that what you write down matches what's on your resume. If you get the job, the client could use this information to buy the cast's wardrobe. Casting directors also need to know if you're available for the shoot dates, and information sheets are a way for you to let them know if you have any conflicts. If there are storyboards or other character descriptions posted, have a look at these, since they can be helpful. After you're signed in, you've read what there is to read and you've got your information sheet filled out, have a seat. Go through a mental checklist of what you prepared to do in the audition room. Run through it once or twice in your head, and try to relax. When it's your turn, your name will be called. Bring your headshot and information sheet into the room and do your thing.

Let's talk about what you can expect from auditions for each of the seven ways (besides theater) actors make a living in Chicago.

Commercials

Most commercial auditions take place at a casting director's office, but some will happen at your agent's office or at an ad agency. As you're called into the room, you'll hand your materials to whoever greets you. At a casting director's office there will likely be at least two people there to watch: the casting director and someone running the equipment. At your agent's office it might just be you and your agent. At an ad agency, there could be a whole bunch of people watching. In any case, you might be given some last-minute instructions which may or may not be completely different from what you were told before. In this business, minds change quickly and if there wasn't time to update the actors, they wait until the audition to do so.

Whether you're auditioning for a speaking role or not, all auditions pretty much run the same way. First, they need to get you on tape identifying yourself so they know who you are. This is called a slate. They might say "Go ahead and slate," or "Let's get your slate." When the camera's rolling you'll look into it and say, "Hi, I'm (your name here)." Sometimes you'll also be asked to say the name of the talent agency that sent you on the audition.

The audition room will be arranged with the camera at one end, pointed at an audition area (which you can think of like a stage) at the other end. If the spot requires a set, a very simple one will be there for you. I use the term "set" incredibly loosely. If the scene takes place at a table, there will be one there with enough chairs around it to accommodate everyone in the scene. That's about as elaborate as these sets get. If you need specific props for the spot, like if you're supposed to talk on a cell phone, the casting director will provide one for you. Don't bring in your own props. When you're ready, you'll do the first take, and hopefully do it much like you prepared it. You'll be told to make some changes and incorporate them into your second take. Based on how that goes, you may be asked to try some other options. Three or four takes usually is the most you'll get. Then you're free to go.

Every actor in nearly every audition is asked to do multiple takes. Don't take this personally. You can't possibly know exactly what they're looking for before you go in, so do your best on the first take and let them direct you for the rest. This doesn't mean you're stinking the place up, it just means you're being brought closer to getting the job. Sometimes they have you do extra takes just to see how versatile you are or how well you take direction.

The one exception to the multiple-take audition model is a style of audition called the interview. Occasionally producers need to see more of your personality than they would find by auditioning you the traditional way. There are roles that require actors to do simple, everyday tasks. Anyone can wipe down windows, use a circular saw to cut a board in half or sit on a couch while typing on a laptop. It's easier for producers to cast these kinds of roles by seeing actors' personalities instead of their mastery of mundane skills. So after your slate, they may ask you a question or two just to see what your personality is like. Sometimes the questions can be related to the spot like, "Tell me about your experience with power tools." Or they can be totally unrelated, like "What would you do if you won the lottery tomorrow?" In any case, producers just want to get a sense of who the actor is and what type they might fit into. Are they pensive, withdrawn and reserved? Or are they open, friendly, and exuberant? Sometimes the decision makers are just trying to find people who sound like they'd be fun to have on a set all day. Other times, they're looking for the actor who will spray the weed killer with just the right attitude. Jobs like these are almost glorified print jobs, so a large part of the casting decision depends on the look they're after. But the interview can be as valuable, or more so, than your look. It's your chance to let people see who you really are, so have some fun with it.

A few years back I had an audition for a furniture maker. The spot took place in a living room, and I was auditioning for the part of the guy sleeping on the couch. I'm not kidding, that was the extent of my role. Oh, wait, I had to shift around a little when the family dog jumped up there with me, but other than that, my job was to sleep through the whole spot. Obviously, there wasn't much for the casting director to have me do except act like I was sleeping, but that's really boring to watch. So in place of that, they interviewed me. I told a story about my dog and the day she ruined the canvas top on my convertible. We were on our way to the groomer. She was seated in the front passenger seat and I was backing out of the garage. As dogs frequently do when they're in cars, she got antsy and started doing her excited-dog-in-a-confined-space dance. She managed to bump the garage door remote on the sun visor with the top of her head, pressing the button to send the door down. I had the radio turned up, so I couldn't hear the door coming down, and the safety mechanism that's supposed to reverse the door when objects (like cars) get in the way wasn't working. So the door came down on top of my convertible as I slowly rolled backward. A nail head on the door snagged some canvas and ripped a nice long hole, which cost me six hundred bucks to fix.

Funny story, right? I later learned that it got me the job. One of the producers on the set told me that I didn't exactly have the look they wanted, but my story made everyone laugh, which made me the ad agency's favorite. That spot ran for three years and paid for a lot of stuff. So that silly little story was much more valuable than my fake sleeping ability. I still tell it whenever I can.

Industrials/Ear Prompter Jobs

Be aware that not every industrial is an ear prompter job. If the job calls for the EAR, you'll be notified ahead of time, and if you're not ear prompter proficient, you won't be included in the audition. These can also take place at various locations: a casting director's office, your agent's place or at the client's office and run in much the same way as commercial auditions. You might be asked to talk a little about your ear prompter experience when you slate, then you'll go into the prepared piece and do your thing. A couple of changes, a second take and you're out of there.

By the way, you should always expect to do the script at least twice. You may have nailed it on the first try, but even if you did, there's always some variation that clients will want to see. Many of them don't know exactly what they want, and they ask actors to help them find out. Their questions usually start with "What if," and the answer comes out in the changes we make to our reads. For example, "What if he thinks the burger is good, but not great?" Well, then the actor doesn't go as big with his reaction when he bites into it. This kind of thing is all part of the process and has nothing to do with you personally.

Voice Over

VO auditions can take place in a couple of locations. Usually it's at your agent's office, but it might be at an ad agency or a recording studio. Some on camera casting directors work on VO projects, but not all that often. There are a couple of casting directors in town that only cast VO.

Scripts are almost never provided ahead of time. Why? The short answer is that it's always been done this way, but I think it also has to do with the nature of the business. Scripts are sometimes rewritten while they're being recorded. The client hears the talent read, and thinks something else would sound better. When this happens, there won't be time for the talent to practice. They'll just have to make the change. Also, sometimes a script isn't approved until moments before it's recorded, so there's nothing to give the talent beforehand. Actors need to be able to do a good job without too much analysis. If you're used to taking a script home and spending a lot of time with it, the VO world will be a lot different.

When you do a VO audition in a location other than your agent's office, you'll walk in, sign in and are handed the copy to look over in the waiting area. Once it's your turn, you'll go into the recording booth, slate and run through it once. You'll be directed and given another take, and then you'll be done. If you stumble or screw up in some other way, you should be given as many chances as you need to get two good takes. This all applies if you're not working out of your home studio. Many agents don't mind if you record the audition at home and send it to them electronically.

Print

These auditions are called "look-see's". Your agent will send you to a photographer's studio. Casting directors sometimes work on print, but not often. You'll bring along a headshot and wear whatever the job calls for, which you'll be told ahead of time. When you get to the studio, you'll sign in, fill out an information card and wait for your turn in front of the camera. Sometimes you'll just have to stand there and smile, other times you'll have to hold some kind of pose. They'll explain the shot to you and walk you through it. Once a few images are snapped, you're out of there. If there are a lot of people at the look-see, we call those cattle calls because it feels like you're just one cow in a huge heard. If you hear people moo-ing, that's why.

Trade Shows/Live Events

These run much like auditions for industrials and happen at your agent's office or at some other location. Casting directors usually don't handle this kind of work. Sometimes these auditions happen at unusual places. I've had to audition at McCormick Place because the client was in town for a different show, and wanted to physically meet the actors rather than watch them on tape. I've also auditioned at a hotel, again because the client was in town. The deal is the same here. You'll do your prepared script, either on the EAR or not, and you'll be given feedback, which you should incorporate into your second take.

TV/Film

Auditions for TV and film roles run the gamut from simple one-liners to full blown scenes. Your script can be a half-page long or ten pages. These auditions nearly always happen at casting director's offices, yet once in a while you might tape at your agent's office. I've done that a few times, most recently to audition for a soap opera. They weren't going to fly me to New York, so I taped it here. No matter where you do the audition, if your scene has other characters in it, someone will be there in the room to read the other characters' lines. Your reader may be an actor who's already cast in a role, or it could be someone from the production company, or even a casting director's intern. They may be great, terrible or somewhere in between. Readers usually try to give you a little something to work with, without taking the focus off of you. After all it's your audi-tion, not theirs. Some readers literally give you nothing. They read the script as if they were reading the nutrition label on a soup can. The casting director, the director or producer of a project, or other production company people may also be in the room. You'll do a take of the scene and then you'll be given direction. You'll incorporate the new direction as best you can for the second take, and if they think you need a third, you'll get one. If not, you're on your way.

Callbacks In Chicago

The organizers of nearly every audition plan for a second one, called a callback. Not everyone gets to do the callback. It's reserved for the actors who seem most right for the job based on what they did the first time around. Sometimes very few actors are called back. I've been one of two people called back. On occasion you're the only one called back for your role, and you're asked to read against actors being considered for the other parts in the project. That's when it's pretty safe to assume you've got the job. Other times, seemingly every actor in town is called back. We call this an "allback", and it simply means the client hasn't a clue what they're looking for. Most often, you're called back with a good number of other actors, maybe a third of those on the first audition. The only kind of work that almost never has a callback is voice over. In all my time as a voice talent, I've done maybe two of them.

A callback works in much the same way as the first audition. Usually you do the same script, though once in a while they switch things up. I've been in callbacks reading a different script, or a revised version of the one I did at the first audition. You can expect more people to be in the room than the first time. These are the decision makers who will choose the talent after they've seen everyone. Typically callbacks are fairly low-key events, but sometimes they can get a little strange from the actor's perspective.

Let's say your callback is for a commercial and it's at a casting director's office. In addition to the casting director and the people they need to run the equipment, the client might also be there. By "the client," I mean it could be one person or ten. Yes, I have walked into callbacks with ten people in the room. Sometimes ad agencies use callbacks as a chance to have a production meeting with whomever they need to meet with about the project. So you're doing your thing in front of everyone and their assistant - the director, the producer, director of photography, the clients (the people who actually work for the company whose product you're pitching), the ad agency creative director, art director, writer, set decorator, wardrobe stylist and anyone else associated with the shoot. And many of them won't be paying you one bit of attention because they're not decision makers about talent, they've got other jobs to do. They'll be on their laptops or smart phones, doing whatever they need to do for later in the meeting when the pesky actors are gone. Don't worry about them, they've got nothing against you, they've just got other things on their mind. The people who need to see your audition will speak up and give you some ideas to chew on before you do your first take.

A far more bizarre situation to be in is the callback that happens while the client is not physically in the room, but on a video monitor, which you look at and talk to instead of a real person. This happens when the client is located in New York or L.A., and is watching your audition on a monitor on the other side of the country. The whole thing is being transmitted over the Internet. The camera that's taping your audition is fed to the client's monitor along with the audio from the mics in your room. The client has a camera and mic on him in his room, which feeds to the monitor in your room. And when you have to ask him a question, you talk to either the monitor he's on, or you look in the camera pointed at you. It's very weird, and it can be tough to forget about and just do your job. But that's what you have to do.

Callbacks work just like the first auditions except you could be asked to do as many takes with as many variations as the client would like to see from you. You can never tell what's going on in their heads, but conventional wisdom holds that when they ask you to do more takes, it means you have a better chance of getting the job. They're trying to see how well you respond to direction, or how many different ways you can interpret the scene. Decision makers like versatility, so the more flexible you are, the better. On the other hand, if you get the old "Great, thanks," after one or two takes, that's a pretty good sign you're not in the running for the job. I don't have any hard numbers to back this up, but I've been told "thanks for coming in," plenty of times after my second take (and sometimes after my first), and I've never gotten one of those jobs. So, from my experience I think conventional wisdom is right in this case.

Unless it's really short, you're not expected to commit a commercial script to memory for the first audition. Casting offices usually have cue cards propped up near the camera. These will probably still be there in the callback, but since second auditions happen a few days to a week after the first one, you would do well to have the script memorized by then. It'll just look better.

Can I Work Now?

Once you've done the callback, how long will you have to wait to hear if you got the job? It depends. It's rare that all of the decision makers are in the room and can, without approval from anyone else, choose talent right after the last actor leaves. It happens though, and if that's the case you could get a call that day. Far more common is the situation where the video has to be viewed by someone who wasn't there, such as an executive from the company whose product you're selling, or a writer or producer on the project who also has a say in who gets hired. It may be a day or two (or more) before you hear anything.

Usually there's one more hoop you have to jump through before the job is officially yours. After the callback, the field of potential candidates is narrowed even further. The next call you get might not be "you got the job," but rather "you're on check avail." Check avail is short for checking your availability. That means that the client has double checked that you're still available on the day of the job, and has put you on notice that they have first dibs on you that day. When you're on check avail they can either book you, which means you got the job, or release you, which means someone else did. Different agents and casting directors use alternative phrases for this. "You're on hold," or "You're on ice," are also ways of saying that the client is interested in you enough that they'd like you to hold the shoot day for them.

This can get confusing, so let's use an example. An actress, Patricia, has been called back for a job that shoots on June 15th. Her callback happens on June 10th, and it goes really well. The next day, June 11th, she gets a call from her agent saying that the client, a software company, wants to put her on check avail. She confirms that she's still available to work on the 15th. At this point, Patricia knows that she's on the short list of actresses who are being considered for the role, but for whatever reason the client hasn't quite made up their collective mind about who to hire. On June 12th, the day after taking the check avail, her agent calls again with news that a past client needs her for a job. This client, a chain of hardware stores, wants to shoot on June 15th, the same day the software company has her locked up. Obviously, Patricia can't be in two places at once. She has two choices: tell the hardware folks she's not available and hope that they'll move their shoot day, or tell the software company that she's got another offer for work on the 15th. Patricia doesn't like the idea of passing up guaranteed work with the hardware company. There's still a chance that she may not be the choice for the software company's job, yet she knows that telling them she's got another offer can cause them to drop her from consideration right away.

There's really no right decision here. Which way Patricia handles the situation depends on the agent's view and Patricia's own conscience. Some agents would say that the chronological order of things should be followed, which means Patricia should tell the hardware client that she's not available on the 15th. Other agents would say that since the software company hasn't given her a firm offer for the job, she's under no obligation to them until they do. Usually the agent would place a phone call to the casting director to try to find out where Patricia stands on the list of actors being considered. Sometimes there are a lot of talent on check avail. If that's the case, Patricia is less likely to get the job than if she was on a very short list. If the agent can find out where she stands, they can make a more informed decision.

Patricia's agent finds out that she's one of many, and after considering all her options, Patricia decides that since she has a valuable on-going relationship with the hardware company, she wouldn't want to jeopardize it in any way. So she and her agent ultimately handle it this way: the software company is told that Patricia has a firm offer for work on the 15th, and they need to make a decision about her, pronto. They have two choices: they can book her or release her. Who knows which way they'll go, but either way, Patricia's working on the 15th.

Guarantees Are Scarce

Being on check avail is a promising step, but it doesn't mean you have the job, so don't do the happy dance just yet. I've been on plenty of check avails and been released plenty of times. My record with one casting office in town was 12 releases in one year. Once per month I was all set to work, then fired before I was even hired. The chosen list of actors still has to reach whoever gets to make the final decision. Once that decision has been made, only then will a call go out to the actor who will be offered the job. If it's you - terrific, your agent will get a call with all the details. If it's not, your agent will get the other kind of call, the one releasing you from that date, and your journey with that particular audition has come to an end.

Do you have to get a callback to get the job? Pretty much. Obviously if the client is planning on casting without a callback, you can book the job by auditioning only once. But if there's a callback and you're not on it, you're not getting the job. Everyone will tell you that you might, but I've never booked a job in that situation, and I don't know anyone who has. Sometimes you're called back but can't go because of another job or an illness. It's too bad, but clients want to see you in person. So if you miss the callback, then it's safe to say that you miss the chance to work.

Alternative Auditions

Remember how I said that your auditions will come through your agent? This is true and it means that without an agent, you don't have a chance at auditioning for the legitimate work that's available to the actors in Chicago. I know you're thinking otherwise, that you can still go after work if you don't have an agent. That's also true, but let me talk about what's available to you when you decide to look for work in this way.

First off, remember that I'm only addressing auditioning for acting work other than theater. You can easily do all kinds of theater in town without having an agent. You might not have access to the big name companies, but plenty of others cast actors without agents all the time. What are your options if you're agent-less?

Craigslist is always the first place people bring up when they talk about auditions they got without an agent. If you don't know the site, visit chicago.craigslist.org and click on the "talent gigs" section to see all the postings. There are people looking for actors, models, musicians, reality show contestants and everything in between. Some postings are quite legitimate and others aren't. You'll find people who are professional (or at least want to be), who will respect you, your time and the process. You'll also find people who wouldn't know professional if it fell out of the sky and gave them a lump on the head. All I'm going to say about auditions you find on Craigslist is that you never know what you're getting into. I've done a few auditions from the site, and I've been disappointed every time, so I don't bother anymore. But I have friends who have had good experiences with Craigslist auditions and regularly peruse the site looking for new opportunities. Just be extra careful and ask a lot of questions before you agree to meet someone to audition. Also, if you get one of these jobs, know that no one is on your side to handle problems or conflicts if they arise. That's what an agent would do. So long as you know that you're on your own and you audition for these jobs at your own risk, you have my blessing to do work from Craigslist. But I've warned you.

A less risky place to find your own auditions are online casting services like Actor's Access and Casting Networks. These are sites used by agents and casting directors in town, so there's a multitude of legitimate auditions posted. Actors can submit themselves for a fee, and I've heard of a few people actually getting booked as a result. But still, unless you have an agent back you up, you need to find out as much as possible about that job before you accept it.

This advice goes for any on camera or voice over audition that doesn't come through an agent. If you find an ad online, in a newspaper or on a bulletin board at a coffee shop, you should approach it with a fair amount of skepticism. That's not to say that all auditions you obtain on your own are going to be bad experiences, but you just have to wonder why the person who needs the actor doesn't call an agent. If it's a money issue, and they think they're going to have to pay too much if they call an agency, there's almost no point in going to the audition at all. You're trying to make a living as an actor in Chicago, right? Why would you give your service away for next to nothing?

I know why – to get experience. You figure that if you get any job, and spend any amount of time on camera or behind a microphone, that will be valuable to you even if you aren't paid. I disagree. It's been my experience, and that of others, that people who bypass talent agents are less experienced in hiring actors, and thus won't have anything to teach you. It's not their fault, it's just that they don't know how to deal with actors. Do you want to donate your time getting this person's project done if you're not going to be paid and you're not going to learn anything? I'd avoid it unless you're really star struck by the project or you're trying to get some tape together for a reel.

Exceptions

Of course, there's an exception to everything. If you know the person you're going to be working for, and you know you're not in danger of having a bad experience with them, do the job. If your uncle Larry needs some VO work done for his company's website, or if you're asked to do a commercial for a family friend that owns a car dealership, go nuts. However, remember that if you're exclusive with an agent, you're obligated to tell the agent about that job and pay them a commission if you get paid. And if you're a union member, you must have the producer sign a union contract for the work.

Tips And Tricks

There are some things you can do in any audition to help you snag the job. They range from the practical to the psychological. None of them will guarantee that you'll get hired, but none of them will hurt your chances either. Incorporating all of them into your routine will help to bring a little order to what can be a chaotic process. Sometimes we're so desperate to get a job that we're willing to try anything in pursuit of success. Usually that's when we fall flat on our faces.

My first suggestion is to plan ahead as much as possible. By that I mean you should do your homework so you can be ready when your name is called. When you get your script, think it through and rehearse it. If you don't know anything about the company or the product, look it up online. Same thing if you don't know the writer or director of a film or TV show. Watch an episode of the show if you can, or read the whole script if you can get it. Simple things like this can go a long way towards being prepared. There's nothing worse than walking into an audition knowing you're going to embarrass yourself because you haven't done any prep.

You don't want to be late. Make sure you leave with plenty of time to get to the audition, park and get inside. If you're rushed, you'll be focused on getting there instead of on what you can do to nail the audition.

Try not to do anything that will call negative attention to yourself. If you're a smoker, let some time lapse between your last cigarette and your audition. You don't want people to smell you when you enter the room. Instead of focusing on your acting, they'll be focused on the odor. And this should go without saying, but I'm going to say it anyway. Never, ever go in to any audition with alcohol on your breath. Sean Bradley of The Green Room tells his students that you should be relaxed and do the audition like you've had two beers, but don't *actually* have two beers before you go in. I once did an audition with an actress who was very good, but reeked of booze. Our appointment time was 1:30 in the afternoon, so she had apparently started on the sauce early that day. I don't remember anything about her, nor do I even recall if I booked the job. I just remember what she looked like and that she smelled like a bar. I'm sure that's what the casting director remembers about her too, and I'm willing to bet she hasn't been called in since.

If you're going to a callback, wear whatever you wore the first time around. Sometimes clients remember you by your shirt color, your scarf or by something else you wore in the audition. So don't give them a reason to ask "Where's the girl in the brown skirt?" Also, don't change what you did in your first audition, do the same thing. They liked whatever you did the first time enough to call you back, so help them remember why they called you back. If you change it up too much, they're going to ask themselves "What's this guy doing? Why is he here?"

Head Games

Go into every audition expecting to get the job. I do this, and it works wonders for my confidence, even when I'm not convinced that I'm right for the role. To me, every job is mine to lose. I just have to help the decision makers see it that way. Don't confuse this with arrogance or cockiness. You don't want to walk into the waiting room and announce that everyone can go home because you're there. But if you approach your auditions with a sense of accomplishment before you've even opened your mouth, that confidence will come through. People are attracted to confidence. Make that natural human tendency work for you.

Whether you're doing a first audition or a callback, walk out of the room, allow yourself ten minutes to think about what you did, then forget about it. Actors are good at mentally replaying their auditions over and over again. We come up with other things we could have done, we think about ways we could have responded differently to direction, and we analyze the reaction in the room. In general, we're good at beating ourselves up over what might have been a great audition. I think it's good to look back on what you did, because you can always learn something from past experience, but too much of this is pointless. You can't change what you did in there. You can't go back and do it a different way. And you really can't read minds, so you'll never be able to tell what the decision makers were thinking. So after ten minutes, take away what you can learn and let it go. This is hard, I know, but it's essential to your longevity in the business. Actors who continuously wring their hands over what they could have done are living in the past and risking burnout. You're better off looking ahead.

Speaking of reading minds, let me remind you that no one can do this. You'll think you can, but you can't. There will be times when you walk out of an audition elated because it went so well. You fit the character description perfectly, your audition was engaging and the clients gave you great feedback. In your brain, you add all these things together and convince yourself that you will, without a doubt, book the job. I've done this.

You'll also walk out of an audition completely and utterly down-trodden by what went on. In this case nothing went according to plan, your time in the room felt awkward and lame, and the clients looked at you with about as much interest as they would if they were looking at a brick wall. You'll leave figuring that not only will you be passed over for the job, but you'll never see the inside of that casting office again because your audition went so horribly awry. I've done this, too.

But years of experience have taught me that you can never tell. Not long ago I had callbacks for two big national spots in the same week. The first was for a discount retailer and it went really well. It was a funny scene between a husband and wife, and I had the clients laughing. I was even asked to hang around and work with several actresses reading for the wife. I left the office thinking, knowing, that I had this job. The other audition was a callback for an automaker. Nothing went right for me. It was a group scene with four actors. My group was filled with models, and I was the only one who had average looks. We were the first group of the day, so our first crack at it was really awkward because no one in the room knew what we should do. Once everyone agreed on a way to shoot the scene, I, the shortest guy there, was placed in the back of the group. I did my thing, got no love from anyone, and the whole thing felt like a waste of time. But it didn't matter, because I had that awesome retail commercial waiting for me in my back pocket, or so I thought. I booked the car spot and never heard from the discount store folks again. I wasn't even put on check avail!

The lesson? You can't read minds, so it's futile to even try. Go in, do your thing, give yourself a few minutes to learn something from what happened and forget you were there. In this business you've got enough cause for emotional gymnastics. Predicting what other people think shouldn't be one of them.

Weird Auditions

While the vast majority of auditions are pretty forgettable, there are times when something happens that's just weird. Not long ago I had a VO audition for a series of TV spots. The product was a drug. Pharmaceutical companies like to hear strong, authoritative, yet friendly voices in their spots, and that's pretty much my thing. I felt really good going into the audition. When I got there the engineer, a friend of mine, said, "They're looking for a Rick Elliott kind of read, so get as close to him as you can."

Now who, you might wonder, is Rick Elliott? Rick is a Chicago-based voice talent who's been in the business a long time. He's a great guy and has a great voice. He's in town and easily available for hire any time, so it's not like he's hard to find. Usually when clients say they want a particular kind of read, it's one a celeb would do. They want a Ryan Seacrest read or a Mike Rowe type, but they don't want to actually hire them. So when I heard they wanted a Rick Elliott sound-alike, I thought, "Why don't they just hire *him*?" I did my best Rick Elliott and forgot about the audition.

About a week later I went back to the same studio to work for a different client, and when I was walking in, guess who was walking out? Yep. I hadn't seen Rick in a long time, so we chatted briefly and I asked him what he was doing at the studio. Of course he was there to do those TV spots. To this day I have no idea why the clients spent the time and money auditioning talent when they knew they wanted Rick. That was just weird and confusing.

Sometimes auditions are so bizarre that they blow my mind. I once had an audition for a bank commercial as a hand model. These auditions are all about gestures since your face isn't in the spot, just your hands. For this one, six actors were brought into the room and the group was split into three pairs. Each pair went through the audition's scenario, which was really easy. One actor handed a couple of hundred-dollar bills to his partner, who took them. Then we switched roles and the first actor received the bills from the second. The camera captured close-ups of the action. After seeing all three pairs go through this super simple routine, there was a pow-wow between the five clients in the room. They decided to have us do a second scenario.

Up to this point this was a fairly typical audition. The only thing that was a little strange was the fact that they used real bills. Usually when there's money in an audition, it's fake for obvious reasons. But then they explained the second deal: they wanted to shoot a close up as we reached out to hold our partner's hands. They wanted to see a comforting gesture as opposed to one that was romantic. So all we had to do was reach out and grab our partner's hand. Fine. Here's where the weirdness started.

Of the three pairs of actors in the room, two consisted of a guy and a girl, but I was paired up with a guy. Now, I'm no homophobe, but this made me uncomfortable. I'm not in the habit of holding hands with other guys. As I'm thinking this, the first group went, and I was able to see the action on the monitor as it was taped. It was a nice, simple, sweet gesture. Next up was me and my dude partner. We both looked at each other, and I turned to the clients and said, "So, this is for the spot you're shooting for the alternative market?" Nervous laughter rippled through the room as everyone realized what was about to happen. We went through with it, but I guarantee that it looked anything but sweet. Obviously not enjoying it, I tried to get it over with as quickly as possible.

I left the room really ticked off. Not because I had to hold hands with a guy, but because there was no good reason to have us do it. There's no way that any bank would ever air a spot with two men holding hands. Like it or not, there isn't a bank executive around that would approve that image in their commercial. So by having that as part of the audition, the client took me and the other guy out of the running for the job right then and there. Why? Because when the tape is reviewed, it'll look horribly awkward, and actors that make clients feel weird don't get jobs. I was ticked off because the client's decision had pushed me down to the bottom of their list before they even looked at the tape! I wasn't given the same shot as the other actors in the room. The only thing good about this audition was that I was paid for it. One of the very few times you'll be paid to audition is when you're up for a hand model job.

The situation could have been handled differently by everyone. Obviously the client could have realized that in this case, asking two guys to hold hands would have been a poor decision and a waste of time. In addition to pointing out the awkwardness, I could have floated the idea of my partner and I pairing up with the two actresses in the room, but by the time I thought of that, the audition was over. The person running the audition could have backed me up when I spoke out about what was about to happen, but they didn't.

A friend of mine told me her weird audition story. It was a commercial audition for a mattress company. The role everyone was auditioning for? The face of a mattress. In the real spot, an actor would put on a specially designed mattress costume, like the kind team mascots wear. The actor's legs, arms, and face would stick out of the getup, so the audition was all about facial expressions. This sounds like a horrible spot, I know, but from what I heard the audition was worse.

Because they couldn't bring in the costume and have every actor put it on, they set up a big piece of Styrofoam with a cutout the size of a head. You know those goofy things at tourist traps with the paintings on one side and steps on the other? The ones you put your face through, and poof! You're a strong man, or a pirate or whatever, and someone takes a picture of you. Like that, only plain white because, you know, you're the face of a mattress. The idea was for the actors to stick their head in this hole, and go through all the facial expressions the mattress would do in the spot. That sounds weird enough, but it was also gross. My friend auditioned near the end of the day, which meant there were tons of other people who put their faces in that cutout before her. By the time it was her turn, there was a ring of makeup around the hole from all of the other actress' faces. Nasty.

Most often you'll be made aware of any weirdness that might come your way. If your audition involves kissing, nudity, smoking or any other action that might make people uncomfortable, you should be told about it ahead of time. This allows you to gracefully back out of the audition before you even get there.

Practice Makes Perfect

I've mentioned that experience is the key to becoming an actor who does great auditions. If you're just beginning or coming back to acting after being away for a while, you should try to get as much practice as you can. You can do this by taking classes. A cold reading class, for example, is a great way to learn how to go on auditions with very little time to prepare.

Early in my career, I took class after class because it was the safest way to discover what worked for me in different situations. For example, it didn't take me long to find out that when I was asked to go off the script and improvise, I froze. Improv wasn't something I was ever exposed to, so I didn't know how to take a script and change it up on the fly. You want to discover your weaknesses where it doesn't cost you anything to screw up, so I took an improv class. Blow enough auditions in the real world and your agent or a casting director will reach a point where they just won't call you again. But in class, you risk nothing. Stay in those classes until you're really comfortable with the entire auditioning process. And even after you reach that point, don't assume you're done learning. Auditioning is a skill, and like anything, it can get rusty if you don't use it all the time. If you go a few months without an audition, you'll be surprised at how unprepared you'll be when you walk into the room. Being away from it for a while can cause you to lose your edge, so don't go more than three or four months without at least being in a class.

If you're strapped for cash and classes seem impractical, or if you're a trained actor who would like to stay sharp, record your own auditions at home. Get yourself a camera, dig up some old scripts and lay a couple takes down on tape. Watch your performance and ask yourself if you'd hire you. The point is that you need to practice this kind of thing if you expect to stay good at it. If you were taking piano lessons and didn't practice, your fingers would lose their flexibility, you'd start to forget your scales and eventually you'd just frustrate the heck out of your teacher. It's the same thing with auditioning. If you let your skills fade, there are plenty of actors who have perfectly brilliant abilities that will get your job.

Finally, the best piece of advice I can give you about auditioning is this: look at it as a chance to do something you love to do. You get to act! Acting is fun, remember? It's why you're in this business in the first place. If you approach the audition process like it's adversarial, you're missing the point. Understand that everyone wants you to do well. No one wants you to fail. In a sense, everyone in an audition room is auditioning for someone else. You're auditioning for the casting director, and you want to do well so that they'll call you in for more auditions. The casting director is auditioning for the client. The casting director also wants you to do well because if you do, you'll make them look good. The client is auditioning for their client, and the client wants you to do well because if you do, you'll make *them* look good. Their client also wants you to do well because if you do, you'll sell the heck out of their product, or TV show or film. So even though it may feel like it's us against them, everyone in the whole process wants actors to do an awesome job every time.

Remember that you love to act, and every audition presents an opportunity to do just that. Walk into the room and have some fun.

CHAPTER EIGHT

Working in Chicago

After you've gotten the agent, gone out on the first audition, nailed the callback and made it through check avail, you're booked! You've been selected as the best person in your talent agency, the city or the country, to play the role you've been offered. First off, congratulate yourself. The odds are always stacked against you getting the job, so you've accomplished quite a lot when you've gotten the call. Be proud of yourself...

But not too proud. After the elation of getting that phone call wears off, now you actually have to do the work. At this point some of you might say, "Holy smokes! I've never done this before." Some of you will say, "Thank the Almighty. I can really use the money." And some will say, "I'm so glad I read Chris Agos' book!" Whatever your reaction, it'll help to know what to expect on the job. Let's look at a typical scenario for each of the seven ways (besides theater) Chicago actors make money.

Commercials

There can be so much variation in this category that it's hard to settle on a set of circumstances you'd "typically" run into. Some shoots last a day, some a week. You could be booked on a job locally or out of town. You might have zero contact with the production company before the job, or you might be on the phone with them quite often. We'll start with the most basic of situations and go from there.

Let's say you've been booked for a spot for an electronics retailer. The spot will shoot locally, and they've scheduled you for one day. As I mentioned before, your agent will give you all of the job's basic information. They'll tell you what day you're shooting, what your call time is (the time you're expected to arrive on the set) and where you're shooting. However, if the production company has more specific information for you, your agent may give them your contact information. They might need your email address to send you any important information, like location maps. Or you might get a call from them. Who's likely to call? The wardrobe people, who will probably want to confirm your sizes so they can shop for you. They may also ask you to bring some of your own clothes to the shoot. You may get a call from the assistant director or whoever is in charge of talent on the project. Sometimes they just want to introduce themselves and see if you have any questions. Other times they have questions for you, and your answers might help the shoot go more smoothly. In our example, let's say they want to double check your height since you'll be standing in front of an LCD TV while you deliver your lines. They want to make sure the TV is positioned right at your shoulder, and if they know your height going in, that will save them time fiddling with the TV on the shoot day. Sure, your height is on your resume, but producers like to be as thorough as possible. That, and they know actors sometimes fib on their resumes, so they want to be certain that they have your actual height instead of the one you wish you had.

In addition to a phone call or two, you should get a copy of the final shooting script. Sometimes scripts are edited between the callback and the shoot, which means you'll have to learn new material. But in this case the final script is exactly the one you did at your callback, so you get off easy. After you have all the information you need and the production company has everything they need from you, there's nothing left for you to do, except show up and do a good job.

The morning of the shoot, you'll be expected to arrive to the location on time. It's important that you do, because any shoot day is usually meticulously planned. Schedules are made up well in advance, and many times there's little room for error. Specifically, the production company doesn't want the cast and crew to go into overtime. This usually happens when everyone's been there for more than nine or ten hours, after which everyone's paid time-and-a-half. Obviously, the extra cost adds up fast. Often this can't be helped, but don't let it be your fault. Be where you're supposed to be and be there on time.

Remember my job for the furniture store? The one where the only thing I had to do was sleep on the couch? I was late to that job. Just like the visit to my first agent's office, I thought I left with plenty of time to get there. But I hit traffic on the expressway. I started getting calls on my cell phone about fifteen minutes after my call time. The assistant director wanted to know when I'd show up and I gave him a guess. The shoot was in an area of the city I had never been in, and once I was in the neighborhood I couldn't find the building. The next time he called I was close to the location. He wanted to know what kind of car I was driving so he could put a production assistant outside on the sidewalk to flag me down when I drove by. Eventually I found the location, pulled over and let the guy park my car. I rushed inside, and got into makeup and wardrobe. When I finally walked onto the set I was almost an hour late. Everyone was nice about it, but the atmosphere was tense, and I knew that it wouldn't ease up until we got rolling and everyone's thoughts shifted from the schedule to the work. By the end of the day I was forgiven, but I really could have done without the stress and anxiety. My lesson: when others are depending on you, make sure they can.

Let's assume you've avoided the drama that comes with being late, and you arrive at the location on time. It's a sound stage the production company rented for the shoot. When you walk in the door, someone will tell you where to park yourself and your stuff. If no one greets you, find someone who looks like they work there. Look for someone that has a walkie-talkie clipped to their hip. Let them know you're an actor, and they'll put you in touch with someone who knows where you should be. Usually your first stop is an area to put your stuff. For our example, say the stage has a green room. You'll drop off your things and head to wardrobe, where you'll get whatever you're wearing for the first shot. If they asked you to bring some of your own clothes, they'll take a look at them, make a decision and tell you to change. When you're in wardrobe, you'll head to makeup, which might be in the same room, but won't be with the same person. A makeup stylist will do your face, so ladies, plan on arriving with your face clean unless you're told otherwise. Some moisturizer is all you need, since anything else will most likely be taken off by the stylist.

The stylist also might do your hair or there could be a different person for that. You might wonder (especially if you're an actress) what kind of style you should go with for on camera work. There's no hard rule, but there are a couple things to keep in mind. Some producers will tell you to show up with your hair completely un-styled. That way, the stylist on the set can do whatever she needs to with it. More often, it makes sense for you to arrive with your hair looking like it did at the audition or callback. If you're someone whose look changes pretty radically when you style your hair a different way, stick with the look you had when they cast you. Ladies, if your hair was curly, don't straighten it. If it was wavy, skip the crazy curly beauty pageant look. Sometimes you'll be asked to come with your hair styled a certain way, which takes away the guess work. Guys, don't get a haircut between the audition and the job if you can help it.

And if you were clean shaven at the audition, show up the same way to the set unless you're told otherwise. They hired you because you had a look that worked for them. If you're just not sure what to do, ask your agent, who can verify what's expected of you.

After wardrobe, makeup and hair, you'll be ready for the day's first shot. This could take place soon after you're ready, or it could be a long wait. I've been rushed onto sets within minutes of being ready, but I've also waited hours between arriving and actually working. You never know what you'll find, so bring something to read. Really. A good book is a great way to fight boredom.

Whenever they're ready for you, you'll be brought to the set by the person who's responsible for you. Sometimes this is a production assistant or some other crew member. They've got another job besides babysitting you, but they'll be your point of contact for the day. If you've got questions or concerns, they're the one to ask. On some jobs you won't have this kind of person, though, and you may have to fend for yourself. But usually someone makes it known that you're to come to them if you need anything.

Once you're on the set, you'll have some time to get familiar with it. There will be lights everywhere, all pointing more or less toward where you'll stand. For our example, let's say the whole stage is painted in an electric green color, and it's empty except for a big flat screen TV on a stand in the middle of the stage. The green paint means that the shot is using a technique called, appropriately enough, green screen. After the shoot, when they edit the piece together, they can drop in digital images on any area of the screen that shows up green. Since the actor, the TV and the stand aren't green, but everything else is, those three things will remain totally unchanged and look just like they would if seen in real life. But thanks to green screen magic, they could look like they're on a beach, floating in outer space or wherever the producers want to put them. You'll probably be shown a mockup depicting what they want the final shot to look like.

You'll be placed where they need you on the set, and that location will be marked with some tape on the floor. This is called your mark, and you'll always need to be standing right on it. The lights will be set specifically for you to stand on that spot and if you're off of it, you'll be out of your light. Same goes for the camera, which will be focused according to your position or else the shot won't work. So it's important to stay on your mark as long as you're needed there.

Let's say your mark is right next to the TV. At this point you'll be visited by the person responsible for recording sound on the job. In my experience, it's almost always a man. The sound guy will place a microphone somewhere in your clothes. This usually involves securing the mic somewhere near your collar, and running the wires down the inside of your shirt and tucking them in your pants or skirt. The idea is to hide all of it. You'll wear a little transmitter somewhere, usually on a belt or waistband in the small of your back. When he's satisfied that the mic is in the right place, he'll ask you to talk a little for a test. I count backwards from ten because, well, that saves me from having to make something up to say. You could also run through your script, but I've found that if you do that on a sound check, everyone suddenly stops and listens to see what the script sounds like when it's said out loud. This could be the first time people hear it, and it gets their attention. Some people listen for your interpretation, or listen to make sure you're saying everything you're supposed to say. But when I'm doing a mic check for the sound guy, I don't want any extra attention. I'm just spitting words out, not acting. I don't want to be scrutinized yet, so I just count backwards and wait to do the script when I'm told.

When the shot is set, the mic is working and the lights are up, it's time to do your thing. At this point the director will take over and have complete charge of the set. If you haven't met him or her yet, you will then. On every job, you'll always start with a rehearsal. This is for everyone: the lighting guys, the camera guys, the sound guys and you.

At this point, the many people standing around will all focus their attention on you, but for different reasons. They'll all be doing their jobs, all of which have something to do with the talent. The lighting guys will be watching to make sure no unexpected shadows or dark spots are present on your face (or anywhere in the shot), the sound guy will be listening for any audio anomalies (like if your mic rustles against your clothes), and the ad agency people (a.k.a. the client) will be paying attention to how the shot looks and how you read the lines. The director is the liaison between you and the client, passing along any comments they might have for you. Once shooting begins for real, anyone in the immediate vicinity of the set will get very quiet so that the mic doesn't pick up anything other than your voice.

This is where it can get nerve wracking for actors, because now it really does become all about you. When the set gets dead quiet and the only one who's allowed to speak is you, it hits home that all the preparation everyone has done up to this point comes down to this: you have to do your job. The lights are hot, you can't move much and the only sound you can hear is your own heartbeat clattering away, betraying your nerves. And then, the director gives you the green light. "Action."

Your experience and training will save you. You can expect the shoot to run much like the callback did. You'll do take after take, making subtle changes along the way until the client is happy with the options they have. Then it'll be over. In our example, you'll stand on your mark next to the TV the whole time. You don't have to walk into the shot or leave it. You'll do your thing, and you'll be done in less time than it took you to get to the location that morning. All that prep for a half hour in front of the camera? Yep.

Our green screen set is a good example of how simple a commercial shoot can be and it can get even simpler. I've done commercial shoots in houses, where a bedroom or kitchen is the set. While the actors are in makeup and wardrobe, the crew is lighting the room, arranging the furniture and putting stuff on the walls to make the shot match the look they want. Then the actor walks in, does his thing and leaves. I've done commercial shoots outside that are even simpler. I once worked on a spot that was shot in a park, and many of the shots were set up about as simply as you'll ever find. A camera on a tripod, one or two lights evening out the natural light from the skies overhead, and that's about it.

Many jobs are much more involved. Usually there are multiple shots scheduled for one day. The crew has quite a bit of work to do in order to set each one up, which means a lot of downtime for you. In fact, it's pretty safe to say that no matter what job you're on, you're going to have a lot of time where you've got nothing to do but wait. This can make the day very long and very stressful if you're new to being on a set. You've done all your preparation, but no one will let you work! You'll spend the day feeling like a racehorse they won't let out of the gate, and all that pent up energy could exhaust you before you ever step in front of a camera. That's why I'm going to mention for a second time that you should bring something to occupy yourself with. I know actors who bring video games, magazines, crossword puzzles and laptops. Most actors are glued to their iPhones or Blackberrys all day long, anything to help them relax and pass the time. Once again, planning ahead will make your day go a lot easier.

The most complicated commercial shoot I've ever done was for a Midwestern state's department of tourism. The goal of the campaign was to attract more people to their state to make it a vacation destination. The ad agency wrote a spot featuring a family traveling around and having fun. I was hired as the dad. Because all the shots needed to be at different locations around the state, the entire cast and crew had to move to each new location for every shot. This meant doing what's called a company move, where literally the entire production and everyone involved with it has to pack up and move to wherever the next shot is located. This is complicated and time consuming. Our spot had three locations separated by hundreds of miles and took four days to shoot. It was a pretty sweet deal for us actors because if we weren't on the set, we were just hanging out in these fun places. We started off at an awesome museum, then headed to a theme park, then finished up shooting in a huge underground cave.

Most commercial shoots are somewhere in between our green screen example and a grand tour of a whole state. Budget is always a concern, so no ad agency or production company would put anything in the schedule that isn't necessary. As you book more and more spots, you'll discover that some shoots are handled more elaborately than others. Depending on what the product is, you could have a bare bones crew with just a few people, or a large crew where even the wardrobe stylist has an assistant. There's really no way to predict what you'll run into on every job.

Whenever you're working out of town, all of your expenses will be paid for by the client. For the tourism job, we were flown in, picked up at the airport and driven to our hotel. As the shoot progressed, we were driven around to each location, and accommodations were taken care of every night. We were given cash for meals, which is called a per diem. If you're a union actor, a per diem when you travel for work is guaranteed by the contract you're working under. Nonunion actors may or may not get a per diem depending on what the agent negotiates. If you're not given cash up front, save all of your receipts to submit for reimbursement later.

In addition to being paid for the job itself, most clients cover just about every expense for the trip. There are, however, some exceptions to this. If you have to park your car at the airport in Chicago while you're gone, you may not be reimbursed for that. Also, you're on your own for anything you buy outside of meals. On the tourism job we had some extra time so we stopped at a cheesy t-shirt shop where I picked up a couple fridge magnets. Reimbursement for travel expenses also goes for when you're working out of town on industrials. Speaking of those...

Industrials/Ear Prompter Jobs

This is another broad category of work that can have a ton of variation from job to job. You can be the only actor on the set or part of a large cast. There are jobs that will require very little work on your part, and ones where you'll have the most work to do of all the actors there. Some shoots will be overwhelmingly complicated, others as simple as can be.

In general, there are two types of on camera industrial jobs: narration and role-playing. In on camera narration jobs, an actor delivers a script while looking directly into the camera as if he's speaking to the audience on the other side of it. That actor is called a narrator or spokesperson. Typically narrators are used to get a company's message across in the most direct way possible, by just telling the audience what the company wants them to know. A video promoting a new product could have a narrator. Role-playing jobs, sometimes referred to as day player jobs, feature two or more actors playing out a scene while ignoring the camera, like what you see in a movie or a play. The audience watches the action unfold as the actors play out the scene. Remember that industrials are typically videos produced for companies. A role-playing job might be two sales people talking about the best way to approach a new customer or a supervisor showing a trainee how to do a certain task.

Very often you'll shoot an industrial at a location that's owned, or otherwise occupied by the company for which you're working. These can vary widely. I've shot industrials in warehouses, greenhouses, paint factories, office towers, call centers, science labs, boardrooms, courtrooms, doctors' offices, car repair shops and parking garages. I've even been flown by helicopter to a farm for a shoot. Most of the work you'll audition for is in the Chicago area, but sometimes you'll work out of town. I've worked in about ten other cities shooting industrials. When the job is officially yours, your agent will have all the details for you. You may have some contact with the production company, especially if the shoot involves travel. Producers like to confirm details like your full name for the plane ticket.

Industrials are interesting because of the opportunity to learn something new. I mean, how would you ever have the chance to learn the process behind making paint? Or how scientists genetically modify corn? Or how you go about selling huge quantities of light fixtures to companies that own skyscrapers? You'd never have the opportunity to know this stuff unless you were in the client's business.

As you work you'll discover that industrial shoots, like commercials, vary widely not only in location and subject matter, but also in complexity. I've had bookings where I was in and out in hardly any time at all. I've also been on shoots that lasted for days. A few years back I was booked to do a driving tour of rural Illinois and Indiana, interviewing farmers for an industrial. The whole crew drove to a farm, put the farmer on camera and talked to him for a little while, then packed up and moved on to the next one. It took nearly a week to get all our work done. There's really no "typical" industrial, but most of them are one to two day shoots. Often, the jobs that are scheduled for one day wind up going into overtime, because it's cheaper for clients to pay everyone a little extra than to bring them back for a second day.

Most times you'll be asked to bring your own wardrobe, so it helps to have a good selection of professional and business casual clothes in your closet. Guys should have one or two pairs of khakis, a few button-down shirts and at least two suits. Vary the colors of what you bring, don't just bring all dark or all light clothing. Women should have the same kind of selection, with accessories and tasteful jewelry to go with their outfits. Remember to stay away from stripes and clothing with visible logos. It's important to follow the instructions you're given to the letter. If they tell you to bring a selection of brown shoes, that means at least two pair. A few choices of whatever you're asked to bring is enough. If you bring your entire closet, you'll just overwhelm them. If you're not married, get a cheap wedding band and bring it with you just in case you're playing someone who's got a spouse. Also, if your real wedding ring is ultra unique or flashy, buy an inexpensive fake ring that's simple and more modest.

It used to be that the majority of industrials hired makeup stylists for the cast. That's been changing as budgets are cut, so don't count on makeup being available at every shoot. Women should ask their agent and arrive to the location with a clean face if makeup is being provided. If not, plan on doing your own makeup and hair either on the set or before you get there. Guys should carry some powder with them to every job, just in case. I've got one compact in my bag that matches my skin tone. I use it fairly frequently, so it comes in handy.

Not all industrials are ear prompter jobs, but you're more likely to use your EAR for industrials than for just about any other kind of work. If you're cast in a production that requires the EAR, you might not get the script until the morning you arrive on the set. Sometimes you get it a day or two ahead of time, and when this happens, usually you're sent a draft they're still working on. They'll hand you the final script on the shoot day. For the producer, that's the advantage of hiring actors that use the EAR. They don't have to finalize the script until the very last minute, which is often when their clients approve it. For the actor, the fact that you don't have to do any memorizing is a huge benefit. It means that you're only working on the shoot day when they're paying you. If you're spending time before the job cramming a script into your head, you're working for free. The EAR allows both actors and producers to be more efficient.

If you're going to use the EAR and you're given the final script ahead of time, don't record it until you get to the job. By all means, go through it to see what you'll be shooting, but don't spend your free time recording unless you're told to do so. There are all kinds of reasons why you should hold off on recording the script. First, you don't know if the script is going to change or not. They might say it's final, but I've gotten rewrites on plenty of "final" scripts. All that time and effort spent recording might go to waste if you have to do it again. Secondly, unless you're given a shot list ahead of time, there's no way to know what order you're going to shoot in. Sometimes scripts can't be shot chronologically. If you record the script from start to finish you might be skipping around all day trying to find the chunk you're shooting next, which is a pain. And if you're on a job with several actors on EAR, there's no good way of recording just your lines only, simply because you never know what you're going to run into on the set. You might need to walk in to the scene, which means you'll have to build in some time at the beginning of your recording. You might have to add some extra time in the middle of a scene to deal with a prop. And you don't know how fast or slow the other actors are going to deliver their lines. There are just too many timing variables, and it's a lot easier to find out what the scene calls for first, then record it with all the elements present. During your EAR training, you'll learn about all of these issues and the importance of timing everything correctly.

The professionals all have two sets of ear prompting equipment. That doesn't mean that if you're new you have to buy two of everything, but if you find yourself doing a lot of work, you should seriously consider buying a backup of everything you use. When you're on the EAR, literally the entire shoot is depending on your equipment working perfectly. And sometimes, recorders crap out. Earpieces can break without warning. Why take the chance that your lack of backup equipment can shut down a whole shoot? If there are other actors on the job, they might loan you whatever you need, but if you're the only one there, you can't go to anyone for backup. Regardless of whether you have backup equipment or not, you should always have spare batteries with you. That goes double for actors with wireless ear prompters. The batteries that those earpieces use are rare, and not something that anyone else on the set is likely to have, so just be prepared and you'll be fine.

Now That It's Over

After you're done with the job, you should try to get a copy of the finished product. Keeping copies of everything you do can be important for a couple of reasons. For one, it's proof that you actually did the job in case the client doesn't pay you. This almost never happens, but it's nice to be able to point to a DVD and say, "See, I did the job," if you have to. Secondly, and probably more importantly, you want to keep copies of your work so that you can string together a couple clips for a reel. If you don't know what a reel looks like, visit www.stewarttalent.com and check out some of the reels there. Basically a reel is a minute's worth of tape showcasing some of the best work you've done in the past. After you have enough work, you can have a commercial reel, an industrial reel, a film/TV reel, etc. This lets clients get a good look at what you can do, and sometimes you can be hired off your reel without an audition. When you're new, you should be collecting everything you do so that you can put together a reel as soon as possible.

Getting a copy, sometimes called a dub, of the finished production can be easier said than done. Commercials can be tough to get because ad agencies don't like to release their work until it airs. There's no telling when they plan on airing their spots, and sometimes even the producers won't know. It's not uncommon for many months to go by between shooting and releasing a spot. And some spots are never meant to be aired. Those are called demos, and they're made to sell an idea to a client, not to be aired as a spot. Dubs of demos are almost never released to talent. Industrials can be tricky to get if there's proprietary information in them that the company doesn't want released to the public. So you may not be able to get a copy of every job, but the only way to know for sure is to ask for one. Don't ask your agent, because that's not their responsibility. It's your job to get your own dubs, so ask your contact person before you leave the job.

After I've been released from the set, I talk to the person who hired me to let them know that I'm interested in getting a dub. If they think it shouldn't be a problem, I'll ask for their contact information so that I can send them a reminder email. I'll offer to pay for any charges the agency or production company would incur by making a dub for me. I'm almost never charged for anything, but it's a nice gesture, since they're sort of doing me a favor by making a dub in the first place. Get your dubs on DVDs if the client doesn't post them online for download. DVDs allow you to easily import the digital files into editing software at home, making the editing process something you can do yourself. Be prepared to wait between two and six months before the final project is available.

Since we're on the subject of what to do when a job is finished, let's cover how you get paid. If you're a union actor, your contact person may or may not have a contract for you to sign when you're done with the job. If one is offered to you, sign it after making sure all the information is correct. If there's no contract on set, keep track of all the details and report them to your agent when you leave. If you're nonunion, you'll likely have a payment voucher to fill out. Every talent agency has their own voucher, but they all basically require the same information: client contact information, job information, and date and times worked. This is the talent agency's only record of the job, so it's important that you fill it out and have your contact person sign it when the job is over. You then have to get it back to your agent in a timely manner, because they'll use it to invoice the client for your paycheck.

Voice Over

VO jobs, if you remember, are jobs where your voice is heard, but you're not seen in the project. Every VO job happens in a recording studio of some kind. It can be one of the large studios downtown, or in a converted closet in a production company's office. I've been to both and everything in between. You might also work at your agent's office (although that's pretty rare), or at your own home studio. If you have a studio in your home, you're an advanced voice talent who can skip down to the next section.

Voice work is great if you can get it, because it usually lasts anywhere from a half hour to a few hours, as opposed to an entire day like on camera work. I've only had one or two VO jobs last for two days, and that was because there was just so much material to record. You don't have to look good or worry about wardrobe for VO work because no one cares what you look like, only what you sound like. And you can make as much money (or more) as an on camera job pays while putting in a fraction of the time.

There are generally two kinds of VO work: spots and narration. Spots are just what you think, radio and TV spots. Most of these jobs are quick unless you're recording several spots at once. Narration is a longer form of VO work, and it can involve reading pages and pages of text for a video, documentary or TV show. As with commercials and industrials, your phone will ring, and your agent will be on the other end of the line letting you know all the details about where, when and who your job is with.

When your VO job is a spot, you'll nearly always head to a recording studio. When you arrive, you'll check in with the receptionist. They'll let the engineer know you're there, and you may have to wait while they get things ready for you. You may or may not be given scripts to look at while you're waiting. If you are, read through them a bit. You might notice that they're similar to the scripts you auditioned on, or they might be different. If they're new to you, do what you can to become familiar with them while you wait. Quietly read them out loud to see if there are any words or phrases that might make you stumble. Everyone has a couple words that are hard to pronounce. For the longest time I couldn't say the word "cellular" clearly. I'd get hung up on it for some reason. I had to get over that really quickly when I was hired to voice a ton of spots for a cellular phone company.

Once you're called into the actual recording studio - "the room" as it's called - you'll meet the clients, who could be the ad agency people that hired you, the producer the ad agency hired to produce the spot, or the folks who actually work for the company the spot is advertising. Figure you'll have one to as many as six or seven people listening in. You'll also meet the engineer, as well as the engineer's assistant if there is one. After everyone's been introduced, it will be time to start recording. You'll be shown into the recording booth, which is isolated from the rest of the room. You'll have the scripts in front of you, and they'll ask you to start reading through the copy for level. This means that the engineer needs to tweak some knobs and dials to get everything sounding good. Once that's done, it will be time to begin recording takes. You'll be directed by whoever is in charge. Usually it's a producer, but sometimes it can be the writer who wrote the spot, or some other person from the ad agency. Occasionally you'll be directed by multiple people.

Sometimes VO jobs use a technology called patching, which allows the talent and the producer to be in different locations, but still communicate with each other. The actor can be in Chicago, and the producer can be in L.A., and the two can talk to each other via the Internet as if they were in the same room. As the actor in a session that's being patched, you'll hear the producer's direction through your headphones in the booth and the producer will be in another studio listening to your takes.

The session will run the same way whether the clients are there with you, or if they're in a studio far away. You'll do a take, it'll be considered and you'll be given some direction for the next take. The process will repeat itself until the producer thinks they have what they need. When you're done, you'll come out of the booth, thank everyone for the work and be on your way. Before you leave, though, you should ask for a copy of the final spot when it's done. Ask the client for it while you're in earshot of the engineer, since it's likely he'll be the one making your dub. Usually the engineer needs to get approval from the client before he releases anything to anyone. So if you ask for a dub right in front of him, you'll save him that step.

I've always found that it's nice to chat with the clients about their product. There can be a little downtime during sessions, and if you ask people about what they're working on, they'll be glad to tell you. But here's a lesson I learned early on: if you shop at their competitor, or you use a competing product, don't bring it up. I was once hired to voice a series of radio spots for Circuit City, a chain of electronics stores that was around a few years ago. These spots were recorded over the course of a few months, and during that time I was in the market for a new TV. One of the sessions was on the Tuesday after the Memorial Day holiday weekend, and in between takes we had a little time to chat. Everyone was talking about what they did for the weekend, and when it was time for me to talk about what I did, I said something like, "I went to all the sales and found an awesome deal on a new TV, and can you believe this, they financed it at zero percent for 24 months! Best Buy sure is great." The room got quiet. After a few awkward seconds one of the producers looked at me and said, "Are you serious?" That was the last session I ever did for Circuit City.

When you're hired for narration, you could be at a recording studio, or you might be at an office with a makeshift recording setup. I've done jobs while sitting on the other side of a client's desk, reading into a mic that's plugged into their laptop. You never really know what you're going to encounter.

As a professional voice talent, you want to show up as prepared as possible. There are any number of things that actors do to get themselves ready for VO jobs. Some do vocal exercises, some sing in the car on the way to the session, some eat an apple right before going into the booth, which helps to eliminate sounds associated with a dry mouth. They do these things partly out of superstition, and partly because their ritual works for them. Personally I don't do anything special to get ready for a job, but there are a couple common sense things that will help make your time in the booth go more smoothly. First, always bring a bottle of water with you to every VO job. When you do a lot of talking, your mouth often dries out. Many recording studios will have water for you, but don't assume that it will be provided. Secondly, try not to talk too much before your session. This goes double for narration jobs, which are longer and require more time than spots. The muscles that allow you to speak can get tired if they're overused, just like any other muscle. When your voice is tired, it shows in your work. If you know you're going to have a long session, do what you can to stay quiet for at least an hour before your call time.

Print

Of all the ways Chicago actors make a buck, print might be the simplest. In its most basic form, a print job requires an actor to be in front of a camera for a little while and then go home. There are jobs that require more than that of course, but many are just that simple. Don't let that make you think it's easy though.

As always, your agent will let you know everything you'll need to do the job. The agent will confirm that your sizes on file are still the same. If they're not, don't lie. Tell the truth, because in most print jobs, clothes that fit well are as important as the actor who acts well.

When you arrive at the photographer's studio, you'll meet the staff that will work on the shoot. You'll be shown to a dressing area, where you'll lay out your wardrobe if you were asked to bring any. You'll also find the wardrobe they bought for you if that's the route they chose. At some point you'll meet the clients, the folks who'll be signing your check. They'll want to talk to you about what you'll wear. You'll try a couple things on and digital stills will be taken of each outfit so that they can remember which they liked the most. Those stills might also be emailed to someone not on site for final wardrobe approval. After the final outfit choice is made, you'll be off to makeup and hair.

A while back I was booked on a print job for a bank. It was for a web banner ad, and the setup was fairly simple except that I needed to appear as if I was trudging up a hill. In the finished ad I would look like I was climbing a huge mountain of money. This mountain must have been really high, because in addition to the incline there was going to be a strong wind knocking me ever so slightly off my footing. This look will be achieved with a combination of real and digital effects. Since it's pretty tough to fake walking uphill, they needed to give me something to help me out with the physical positioning.

When I walked onto the set, I saw that they built a ramp out of plywood. The thing was about four feet tall. The idea was for me to stand on it and lean forward a little during the shoot, which helped me really look like I was walking up a hill. I climbed on in my dress shoes, which made the plywood slippery. It was a little tense at first because I kept sliding down the stupid thing. Once I found a standing position that I could keep without the fear of toppling over, things got more interesting. They turned on a fan to blow my hair and suit around to simulate a headwind. Unfortunately it also made me feel like I was going to slip and fall.

After a few lighting tweaks and practice shots, the job was underway. The pace dramatically quickened, with the shooter grabbing shot after shot in rapid succession. As the photographer snapped away, the client was able to see the images as they were processed by a computer. They came up fairly quickly, and each was considered, scrutinized, and evaluated. During this time, I was told what to do by many people at once. By the time it was over, my legs were killing me from straining to hold a position, and I was really ready to get down off that goofy ramp.

Print jobs are only about one thing: how you look. So there's much more scrutiny of your physical appearance than in any other kind of work you'll do. You'll be told to shift your weight, stand up straight, bend over slightly, lift your right hand, rotate your left hand, tilt your head one way (then another) and try a variety of facial expressions. This is just the tip of the iceberg, who knows what other directions will be hurled at you. Traditionally the photographer acts like the director and tells the talent what to do, but these days, with clients being able to see the images as they are created, input comes from many people. Do your best to keep up with all of their suggestions.

Every print job ends for the actor after the client gets the look they're trying to achieve - that point could come after 100 images, or many, many more. The thing to remember is this: your job is to do what you can to give them what they need while you're there. It can be frustrating taking so much direction, especially for seemingly unimportant minutiae like how tightly the fingers on your right hand are curled, but that's the job of the print model, and they're paying you good money to do it. It can also be tiring holding an awkward position for a long period of time. What can I say, eat a good breakfast so that you have enough energy to get through the day.

My time on the plywood ramp is emblematic of the way print ads are put together these days. Photo editing software is used to create the great majority of print ads. The ramp would be cropped out of the image, and you would be digitally placed on top of the pile of money, which would be either digitally created, or shot separately. The fan saves the editors from creating the effect of wind rustling your hair and clothes with computers after the fact. It's rare to set up a whole shot photographically these days without digital assistance.

Sometimes, one photo shoot isn't enough to get it right. Very early in my career I was hired to do some product packaging for a company that supplies wedding products. Cake toppers, decorations, reception giveaways, stuff like that. They cast me as a groom, and the shot of me and my bride was to end up on a box of bubbles, the kind given to guests so that they can blow them toward the bride and groom as they leave the ceremony. The setup was really easy. I brought my own tux, which I owned only because I had to have one for choir concerts in college (I think this is why I got the job in the first place) and they stood me and the wife in front of a pale blue background. We held hands and smiled, pretending that we were just married and by the end of the shoot, everyone was happy with the result.

A few weeks later, my agent called and said they wanted to shoot a second time. They liked what I did, but weren't happy with the model who played my bride. When I got to the second shoot, there was a different girl waiting to hold my hand. We did the whole thing over again. About a month went by and I forgot about the job, figuring that it was over. It wasn't. My agent called again and told me they hoped the third time was the charm. I have no idea why they passed on either bride, but I didn't care because I was going to get paid three times. As far as I was concerned, they could marry me off to every model in the city. The third shoot was in a totally different location. It was outside in front of an actual church, whereas the second shoot had some kind of background behind us that looked like fake stained glass. There was one little problem, though. This bride was at least two inches taller than I am, which didn't look right. Apparently no one had done the math when they hired her, so the photographer had to think on his feet a bit. In order to make me look taller, they put me on her right side, which was in the foreground of the image. They also gave me something to stand on, boosting my height. The tricks worked, and this time they were even happy with the bride! The final image was on thousands of boxes of bubbles sold at Wal-Mart for ten years. It was only recently replaced with an updated photo of two other young newlyweds.

Getting a copy of your print work can be even more frustrating than getting commercial or industrial work. It can take months for projects to be finished, and it can be that long before you can get a copy. These are called tear sheets, and they can be anything: a newspaper ad, the front of a cereal box or a page out of a catalog. Whatever the shoot was for, the final use of that image is a tear sheet. Sometimes, like with the bubbles, you can find them on your own if the project has been released to the public. Other times you have to go through the photographer. This can take a long time, but it's worth the effort. If you find yourself doing a lot of print work, it'll be a good idea to put together a comp card for that work. Comp is short for composite, and it's a small collection of different looks you're able to pull off, printed on a card about the size of a half sheet of paper. Generally one side has one large image of you, the best one you have, and the other side has a series of smaller images. Sometimes these are actual examples of your work, which is why getting tear sheets is a good idea. Plus, it's just fun to see what your time and effort turned into.

Trade Shows

Are you getting the feeling that I'm going to tell you that trade show jobs are just as varied as commercial, industrial, voice over and print jobs? You're catching on to one of the main characteristics of this business. Unpredictability rules the whole industry from top to bottom. It doesn't matter if you're the highest of A-list Hollywood talent or the least experienced actor in the nation's third largest market. You'll never know what the next job holds for you, and that includes trade show work.

As you read earlier, you could be hired to work a show as a host, crowd gatherer, product specialist or presenter. You could also be hired as a combination of all four. Once again, your agent will give you all the details.

Trade show work frequently brings actors to cities other than Chicago. Big shows are held in Vegas, Orlando and New York, as well as other cities, like San Francisco, Philadelphia and Detroit. A friend of mine has even worked as a narrator internationally in English-speaking markets. Your travel expenses will be covered by the client. While some shows have been leaving Chicago recently, there's still plenty of work here from clients both large and small. Small companies like to hire local talent when they're in town because that saves them the cost of flying people in and paying to lodge them for the duration of the show. Large companies that do many shows throughout the year like to hire teams of actors to travel with the shows, heading to each city as the year progresses. When you audition or otherwise interview for the job, you'll be told which kind of system they're looking to plug you into.

It's very common for Chicago actors to be hired to do a single show locally. The show may last as long as four days, and you may be needed on all of them or just one. Let's say you're hired as a presenter for a show at McCormick Place. A small company is coming into town and they'd like you to do a presentation showcasing their latest product. Your script is roughly eight minutes long and will happen every hour on the hour, every day of the show. You've auditioned for it, made it past the callback and have been told you're the one they want.

You can expect the job to start with a rehearsal day, usually the day before the show opens. Most often you'll be given the script before the rehearsal, but it's possible you won't see it until you first meet the clients on the show floor. If that's the case you'll be expected to lay the script down on your EAR for the rehearsal. That's a good way of discovering what challenges await you. In our example, let's say you have to time the script to a video, which the client has already produced. You'll spend much of the day fine tuning the timing between your live presentation and the recorded elements. If there's a product demonstration, you'll also work on learning how to handle whatever they want you to do in that capacity. Hopefully by the end of the day, you'll have most of the kinks worked out.

The day the show opens, expect your call time to be very early in the morning. Usually clients like to see one final rehearsal before you do the presentation for show attendees. This gives you a chance to work on any changes you might have made toward the end of the previous day, and gives the client the chance to work out any technical issues. Don't sweat it if the morning's run-through isn't perfect. The more complicated the presentation is, the longer it will take to get it up and running. Don't be too relaxed though, because at some point, as the saying goes, the show must go on. Often there's a meeting of the entire booth staff on the morning of the first day of the show. This is usually your first audience, and it's a friendly one. It will probably be your last chance to get all the kinks worked out before you do the presentation in front of people who might do business with your client.

Once the show floor opens and your client's potential partners and customers start strolling through the aisles, you'll do your thing on a set schedule. When you're not speaking, you'll be off. So if your presentations are every hour on the hour and they last for a few minutes, the rest of the time you're free to do what you like. You might be asked to hang around and help connect show attendees with questions to company reps who can answer them.

Working only eight minutes an hour sounds great doesn't it? Remember – bring stuff to help you kill time. Unless you're interested in the subject of the show, there's going to be nothing for you to do for a good part of every hour of the day. I shopped for and bought my wife's engagement ring while I was working a trade show for Toyota. The show was in

Millenium Park, and my presentation was every hour on the hour. It only lasted about ten minutes, which meant the rest of the hour was mine. So I'd take the five-minute walk to Jeweler's Row on Wabash and shop for diamonds. I think I bought one on day four of the show.

Eventually, you'll settle into a rhythm and be able to knock off the presentations in your sleep. You're going to do the same script over and over again with no variation, every hour on the hour for as many as four days. Or possibly every half hour, which would mean that you could do sixteen shows a day. You'll be given time off for lunch, but you can see that trade show narration work can be extremely repetitive and downright mind numbing if you're not into the subject matter.

The job I just described is a simple one: one actor, one video, one presentation. Sometimes there are multiple actors, multiple scripts, multiple product demos and multiple people to keep happy. The most complex trade show I've ever done was for the Food Marketing Institute, a trade association that supports the grocery store industry. The job became known as The Mother of All Trade Show Presentations, and for good reason. It involved 11 actors doing a show that was 30 minutes long, and was so complicated that at first it seemed that disaster would be the only possible outcome. All eleven of us were on the EAR, and we not only had to time our delivery to each other, but also to video, lighting and sound cues.

As if that wasn't hard enough, the cast was split up and put into different "theaters". The audience would begin in one theater where they'd be greeted by the first actor, who explained to them how the presentation would work. Then they would walk through the other theaters while a different scene would play out in each one. When they walked into a room, the lights went up, our microphones went live and a video began playing. Many scenes involved actors interacting not only with each other, but with the video and props as well, so timing was a huge issue. The video that ran on every screen in every theater was run by a guy backstage, but it was one long piece that started when the audience was in the first theater and ended when they were walking out of the last one. The guy pressed the play button only once, when the audience was in their first location, not when they entered each theater. The lighting and the mics were all automated and timed with the video. This meant that there was no room for error. Each actor had to start their EAR at just the right time. Too soon and the audience wouldn't hear anything because your mic wouldn't be on. Too late and you'd be behind the video and lights, which meant that at the end, you'd finish your scene in darkness and silence and the audience wouldn't know what was going on.

The process was like a big, momentum-gathering machine. By the time one group was finishing up, the next would be starting at the beginning. There was no stopping midway through. Every actor had to be aware of where the group was, because they had to be in place when their part of the presentation was about to begin. Only once did an actor miss his cue by a few seconds because he was late coming back from the restroom.

It was exhausting, but by the end of each day it was really gratifying. I knew that I was part of something that was really unusual, and I was right. The presentation's sponsors followed up with other, smaller ones in later years. The year after that monster job, they tried a similar concept but with far fewer actors, only five. The year after that, it was just me on my ear prompter, timing my presentation to a single video. These days they don't even hold the show in Chicago anymore. I've never heard of a job quite like that first year, and with today's shrinking budgets, I don't think it'll ever happen again. But it gives you a good idea of how trade show work runs the gamut of complexity.

Some presentations are videotaped for future use by the company. If this is the case, your agent should negotiate another payment for you to cover the video. If they're shooting just for archival purposes, your agent might not be able to get anything for you. Either way, try to get a copy of that footage. It'll come in handy if you want to put together a trade show reel. By the end of the show, you'll know whoever hired you pretty well. Just let them know you'd like to have a copy for your own personal use, and they should be able to get a dub to you. Again, tell them you'll pay for it. You probably won't have to, but it's nice to make the offer.

TV/Film

There's nothing quite like getting the call that you're the choice for a role in a film or TV show. For most of us in Chicago it doesn't happen often, and it's a special feeling. Competition is tough for these roles, and if you're the one, you really did something right in the audition room. Unfortunately, doing the job is usually not as exciting as getting the phone call that you got it.

Working on a big budget film set is an exercise in waiting. Let's say you booked a role as a bartender, and they'll need you for one day. As you might expect, your agent will have the details for you, but there's almost always a phone call or two from the production folks. You can expect your call time to be very early in the morning. In some cases, you may be offered a pickup from your home and be driven to the shoot location, but most often you're expected to get to the set on your own. When you arrive, you'll be introduced to whoever is handling talent, sometimes the second assistant director or some other crew member. It will be important for that person to know where you are at all times because they'll be responsible for getting you wherever you're supposed to be. The first place you'll go is to your green room if you're shooting on a sound stage or to your trailer if you're out on location. And you could be there a very, very long time. Hours, in fact, without any contact from your handler, who might be busy with other tasks.

The call sheet will give you an idea of what your day will be like.

You'll be given one in the morning when you arrive, and on it will be all the information for the day's shoot. All the actors and their roles will be listed there, along with their call times and the shooting schedule. The sheet will have all kinds of other information as well, like the weather forecast, the crew listing and a list of special equipment needed to shoot the day's scenes.

Along with the call sheet you'll be given the script for your scenes. These are called sides, and they may have changed since you saw them at the audition, so you'll want to have a look and get familiar with the new material if there is any. Sometimes they give you more lines or they may take some away. Be ready for either.

Let's say your call time is 7:00 a.m., and you arrive on time. By 7:15 you'll know where you'll be sitting and waiting for your turn to work. By 7:30, you might be done catching up on the changes in the script. By 8:00 you'll be emotionally ready to go. You might even be changed into your wardrobe since it's usually placed in your holding area before you arrive. But the call sheet says you're not on until noon. That means you've got four hours to hang out and wait for your moment in front of the camera, and it could take longer than that. Often shooting takes longer than expected, causing you to wait even longer before you work. It's a challenge to stay focused and energized while you wait, but that's your job. Some actors take a nap and others bury themselves in books or iPhones. However you deal with it, your job is to show up to the set very ready when they're ready for you. Around 11:00 a.m., in anticipation of shooting your scene, you're told to go to makeup and hair.

At 1:00 p.m., lunch is called, which means that everyone will eat before you get to do your scene. It'll be at least another hour before you're called to the set. Lunch is always provided, and just about everyone eats at the same time. So you'll eat before you work, even though the call sheet says you were supposed to shoot before then. Finally, after killing as much time as you've ever killed in one day, the second assistant director comes to get you. It's time.

You'll be shown to the set, which in our example is a bar. Once you get on the set, your handler will step back and you'll be in the hands of the first assistant director and the director, who will tell you where your position is for your first setup. You'll also meet the other actors if you haven't been introduced already. (Here's a tip: if you're working with someone famous, act like you've been there before and don't get all star struck. They're just people, and they put their pants on one leg at a time just like you.) There will be rehearsals, which are as much for the lighting and sound guys as it is for the cast, and when everyone's ready, shooting will begin.

Shooting will go just like any commercial or industrial. They'll do multiple takes, stopping between each one to make adjustments as needed. In fact, if you're nervous about working on a big job like a film, just look at it like a big industrial. Listen to the director and change your performance up as much as they ask. If they're shooting with only one camera, they'll shoot what's called a master shot first. That's a shot that includes as many actors in the scene as possible. After they're happy with the master, they'll move in for coverage, which means they'll shoot close-ups. When it's time for your close-up, do the scene as you did it in the master shot, and change it up if asked again. Once all your scenes are shot, you're released and free to go home. You'll change out of your wardrobe, give it back to them, and be on your way.

The process in our film example is the same if you're shooting an episode of a large budget TV show. But if you're working with smaller budget projects, you should adjust your expectations a little. There may be less people working on the set. There might be no one to do hair or makeup. There might not even be a call sheet if you're working with a very small and informal indie film production. Once you really get down to the point where everyone's working for free, you'll be asked to bring your own wardrobe and maybe a prop or two. Chicago hosts productions up and down the pyramid, and when you audition for the role you'll know what kind you're dealing with. If you found the audition notice on Craigslist, you should expect to find a very stripped down production where everyone who's there is doing it for experience or doing someone else a favor.

You'll definitely want to get a copy of whatever film and TV work you get, though you'll have to wait until the movie or show is released. Then you can buy the DVD or record it on your DVR like everyone else, or get it from the producer if it's an independent low-budget project. Having a film/TV reel is a great way to make sure you're considered for that kind of work.

The working conditions you're likely to run into while shooting TV and film depend largely on whether or not you're working on a union set. All large budget Hollywood-based productions are union, as are many smaller independent films. There's some TV being shot in Chicago that isn't union, though they're mostly reality shows. Some ultra-low budget films sign agreements with the unions, even though they really can't afford to pay union rates. The agreements make the producers promise to provide good working conditions if they cast union actors. They also allow producers to pay actors on a deferred basis. In these cases the actors aren't paid much unless the film gets distribution. This is a way for producers to be able to use union talent, and it provides more work for actors. When a union actor works on one of these productions, they don't do it for the money. It's more about the experience and the footage for their reel.

If you work a nonunion film or TV project, there's isn't a set of rules the producer has to follow. That's not to say that all nonunion productions are going to work you to death and make you wish you never signed on to the project, but there's nothing to say they won't either. There's absolutely nothing wrong with working on a nonunion production as long as you're not a member of a union. Just be aware that you're on your own for everything.

Unions play a very important role in this business, and you should try to get to know as much about them as possible. The next chapter will give you a good start.

CHAPTER NINE

The Actor's Unions

Late on the last night of an on camera class I was teaching, a student raised her hand and asked a question about unions. I gave a quick answer and started to move on to whatever I had planned for the rest of the night, but someone else asked a follow up question. Then more hands went up. A long discussion followed, which lasted well past the end of class. As much as I wanted to think they couldn't stand to say goodbye to me, the students were finally getting answers to questions they've always wanted to ask. They wondered if unions guarantee that actors will work. They were curious about getting into a union, whether unions act like employment agencies, about union pay rates, and about the need for unions at all. I wasn't surprised by this. In fact, when people ask me about the business, they're either trying to figure out a way in, or they're asking some union-related question. Clearly there's a need to explain what the heck unions are and what they do.

The big question most actors ask at one point or another is: Should I join the unions? The answer is different for everyone, and I have my own view on the subject. But before I tell you what I think, I'm going to tell you everything you need to know about them so you can answer that question for yourself.

The Screen Actor's Guild (SAG) and The American Federation of Radio and Television Artists (AFTRA) are the two unions that cover actors who work in the world of on camera and voice over. Actors pay dues, and the unions use that money to pay for lawyers who work out collective bargaining agreements with producers. These negotiations result in contracts, which spell out rules that both producers and actors agree to follow on a job. The rules are designed to protect actors and address everything from pay rates, to working conditions, to health care. The unions don't negotiate for you individually, but for the entire membership. The contracts negotiated on your behalf are the same ones all union actors work under. These contracts only apply to broadcast TV, film, commercial, radio, web and industrial work. There are no unions that cover trade show or print work. Stage work is covered under Actor's Equity Association, a union that isn't relevant to our current discussion, so we'll skip it.

A lot of people outside the business wonder why SAG and AFTRA even exist. They hear about stars making $20 million a movie, and they assume that if actors make that kind of money, they can do just fine on their own. The reality is that the vast majority of actors don't make anything near those headline-grabbing fees, and they rely on the unions to negotiate pay and terms that can help them earn a living wage from acting.

But there's another reason why unions exist, and that's because of the nature of the business. Acting is the kind of thing so many people want to do, that many would do it for free. Think about it. If you were given a chance to work with some really famous people and possibly launch your career and become famous yourself in the deal, would you do it for nothing? After all, once you're famous, the money thing usually takes care of itself. So why not take the offer to be in that movie even though you're not going to earn anything for it? You'll probably be paid some other way on some other day, but you'll have the chance to make a dream come true. You'll be a movie star, which is a pretty alluring thought. Maybe enticing enough that you'd skip a paycheck to make it happen, or maybe not.

Plenty of people would take this deal and hope for the money to show up later. If enough people did that, there would be no way that actors at any level would be able to make a living, because producers would expect everyone to work without pay. That would make the going rate for an actor's service a big fat zero. No one can afford to spend all of their time working for free; actors have to do *something* to make money, and this would leave no time in their schedule to act. So what do you think would happen? There would be no professional actors, which means there would be no movies, TV shows, commercials, agents, producers, or production companies. The unions exist because without them, show business as we know it wouldn't really exist. We'd just have a bunch of unprotected people who spend all their time hoping instead of earning.

As a side note, I want you to remember something. Nobody works for free. Repeat those words to yourself if you're ever approached by someone wanting to use your services and claims to have no way to compensate you. If you're willing to work for free, you're not making a living, you're begging. Some projects need actors, but have very limited budgets. That's fine, but get something from them; if not money then make sure you're fed, or you're getting a copy of the finished work for your reel, or you're given some other form of compensation. Never devalue your skills by giving them away. Once you do, you might find it difficult to start charging for them again. End of rant and back to the subject at hand.

The idea behind a union is to give employees (actors) the power to negotiate with management (producers) as one large group instead of individually. There's safety in numbers. If you have a whole lot of people saying, "We need things to be done this way," that carries much more weight than if one person takes a stand. So the unions are there to level the playing field and give all actors a chance at making a living in exchange for producers using the services of actors to generate income for themselves.

Why are there two unions and not just one? That's a question many people ask, and in the past there have been efforts to unite the two under one umbrella. But for a variety of reasons, this hasn't happened. Until it does, actors are left with two separate groups to join. In the past they each covered different kinds of work. SAG covered anything shot on film, and AFTRA looked after anything shot on video and recorded for radio. Rapid advances in technology coupled with steep declines in production costs have changed the way producers shoot. These days, almost everything is shot digitally, leaving both unions to cover more or less the same kind of work. SAG still covers projects shot on film, but also handles those made using any other digital media. This includes movies, TV shows, commercials, and projects shot for the Internet, like webisodes and other electronically distributed content. All the famous Hollywood actors are members of SAG, so if you join, you'll have the same membership card as Tom Hanks and Julia Roberts. SAG also covers voice over work in TV spots, so if you're the announcer in a SAG commercial, that job will fall under SAG too.

AFTRA covers anything shot on electronic media as well, but is still the only union representing actors doing radio spots. Just like with SAG, if you're a voice talent working on an AFTRA project with an on camera component (like doing the voice over narration on a video), that job will be covered under AFTRA. Since they both cover the same kind of work, how is it decided which union covers which job? Basically it's up to the producer unless it's radio. In that case it's definitely an AFTRA job, but if it's anything else, it could be covered by either union.

Both unions work together when contracts are up for renewal, but that's pretty much where their partnership ends. Since they're separate entities, they each have their own initiation fees, dues structure, health and retirement plans, policies and procedures. This means that when you join one, you're not automatically a member of the other. If you're thinking ahead, you've figured out that you'll have to pay two initiation fees and two sets of dues. You also may qualify for two health and retirement plans. Now you can see why the subject of unions can be complicated.

A lot of nonunion actors think that once they join the unions, they'll have all the work they can possibly handle because the unions will see to it that they're kept busy. They assume the unions work like temp agencies, finding work for actors and placing them in those jobs. This isn't true at all. Being in SAG and AFTRA does not guarantee that you'll get work. You still have to audition for jobs and be selected by the producer. A union's job is to protect a member's interests while they're on the job. It's still up to the member to get the job in the first place.

In exchange for that protection, the unions expect their membership to only take union work. It's important to keep in mind that not all jobs available to Chicago actors are union jobs. Producers have to actively make the decision to hire union talent or not. There is plenty of nonunion work. Before you audition for any job, you'll need to know ahead of time if it's a union booking or not. You'll see why later in this chapter.

Joining SAG And AFTRA

Before you have to worry about fees, rules, and what unions do, you have to join one. Each union handles the process of joining differently. SAG generally requires actors to be cast in a SAG production before they can join. Since any SAG job is usually only open to SAG members, actors have forever been frustrated by this catch-22 wondering, "If I have to be union to work the job, but I need the job to become union, how am I ever going to be able to join?" This is a fair question. While producers of union productions usually just want to audition union performers, sometimes they're open to seeing nonunion actors, too. Casting directors, agents and producers just want to put the best actor for the role in the job, and if a nonunion actor is the choice, so be it. I broke into SAG like a lot of other actors, by doing a commercial. I was hired to voice a spot for Pepto Bismol. I was doing all nonunion work at that point, but I was with an agent who worked with both union and nonunion jobs. She put me on the audition and I shocked her by getting the job. If you're looking to join SAG, you'll have the chance every time you audition for a SAG production.

But getting cast in a SAG job isn't the only way in. There are two other ways they'll let you join. You can join if you work as an extra on a SAG commercial for three days. SAG also accepts actors who are members of other performance unions, including AFTRA. If you've been a member of AFTRA for at least one year, and during that time you've been hired in a principal role (not a background role) in an AFTRA production, you're good to go as far as SAG is concerned.

Becoming a member of AFTRA is simple. You bring them a check for the initiation fee and sign some paperwork, and you're a member. They don't make you jump through the employment hoops like SAG.

Taft-Hartley Is What?

No matter which union you're interested in, you don't have to join immediately upon getting your first union booking. There's a federal law called the Taft Hartley Act that regulates labor unions. This law allows you a month between when you work your first job and when you have to join the union. Consider it a time to test drive what it's like to be a union actor.

Let's say you work your first SAG project on June 1st. You're now in a new phase of your career. You're no longer strictly a nonunion actor, you're what's called "Taft-Hartley'd" for SAG. Starting June 2nd you can work as many SAG jobs as you can get for thirty days without joining. However, once that thirty day period ends, the free ride is over. After June

30th, you must join if you want to work another SAG job. This rule also applies for AFTRA, however SAG has an additional special provision called "OK-30" that will buy you another thirty days of work without having to join. Your agent has to call the union office and ask for it to be applied in your case. With AFTRA there's no such provision.

Many actors work their first union job and then don't book another one during their month of freebies. In fact, some actors wait years to join. This might be because they don't really want to join, so they avoid union auditions. Or it could be that the stars haven't aligned for them, and they're still waiting to be offered their next union booking. It doesn't matter how long it takes between your first job and the one that forces you to join. During that time you're considered Taft Hartley'd for either AFTRA or SAG, or both of them. Your Taft-Hartley status never expires until you join.

You might be wondering how the union knows who works on what job. They have two ways to find out. First, producers are supposed to call the local union office before they officially hire an actor to verify that the actor is eligible to do the work. What makes you ineligible? Falling behind on your dues. So if the union tells the producer that an actor is not eligible to work, that actor will lose the job before he even knows he had it. That's why you always want to pay your dues on time. Not every producer makes that call, though, so the union relies on a second method of knowing who worked a job. Every producer who hires union actors has to file payroll information with the union. The producer's paperwork is used to make sure you're being paid the correct amount. So the union gets a list of every actor who will be paid under the union contract, and they check the names against their list of current members and Taft-Hartley'd actors. If you want to be paid, there's no slipping through the cracks.

Once you're beyond your freebie period, you'll have to join the union before working your next job. This can cause quite a panic for a couple of reasons. First, you never know when you're going to book your next union job. Let's say a producer decides to cast you on a Thursday afternoon at four o'clock. That's great, except the job shoots on Friday starting at 7:00 a.m. If they call the union office to verify that you're eligible to work, and you're past your 30-day freebie period, the producer will be told about your status. You're what's called a "must join." That means you have one hour to join the union, because the office closes at five o'clock and won't re-open until 9:00 a.m. the next day. The producer will call your agent, who will call you and let you know both the good and the bad news. You got the job, but you'll have to arrange to join the union before you can work it. Stressful, eh? Secondly, as if that wasn't bad enough, the initiation fee for both unions is substantial. So now you have to come up with a good chunk of money on very short notice.

How do you deal with all of this? Most often, you're required to be physically present at the union office to join. However for situations like the one described above, SAG has a grace period. You can work the job, but you'll have to join within the next five business days. AFTRA, on the other hand, has no grace period, but allows you to join online, so you can take care of it after hours if you find yourself needing to join ASAP. What about the initiation fee? You can't really predict when you're going to book the job that forces you to join the union. So my advice is to save up the cash, and have it readily available at a moment's notice.

The example I gave above is pretty extreme. When I joined SAG, I was lucky because I had about a day's notice. I got the call on Wednesday that I had a booking on Friday. So Thursday I went to the bank, grabbed a cashier's check and took care of business. I did this twice, once for SAG and another time for AFTRA. Both times I joined because I had a good job waiting for me. Back then you had to pay the entire initiation fee at once. Now, there's a payment plan available and the unions accept credit cards. If you find yourself short on cash when you need to join, the union's office staff will have all the details.

Becoming a union member is a rite of passage and a source of pride for many actors. To some, being in the union means that they've arrived, and they're really a professional. Before you consider whether or not union membership is for you, it'll help to know what it's like to be a union actor, and how that differs from being nonunion. I'm going to break it down into two sections. First, I'll talk about the things you can expect from being a union talent. Then I'll tell you about what life is like as a nonunion actor. After learning about both, you'll have a better idea of what you want for your career.

Life As A Union Actor

Once you're past all the drama surrounding whether or not to join, you're out in the world working as a card-carrying union actor. Being a member of AFTRA or SAG has a lot of advantages, most of which center on money. To begin with, the union makes sure that actors are well compensated for their work. As a union actor you have the opportunity to earn money while you're not even working. That's due to an aspect of the contracts called the residual system. When you book a job on a commercial, film or TV project, you're paid for your time on the set. That's called a session fee, and it covers whatever time you spent physically on the job. Most union jobs are billed by the day with the exception of voice over jobs, which are billed by the hour or the spot, depending on the job. On top of the session fee, the producer has to pay you a usage fee. In other words, they're buying a license to use your face or voice for a set period of time. That usage fee is called a residual payment. Actors just refer to them as residuals. This is essentially money you get for doing nothing.

Say you're booked for one day on a commercial. The SAG/AFTRA commercial contract guarantees that you'll be paid a certain amount for that day, and no lower. The lowest possible rate is called the scale rate.

Actors just say they're working for scale. That rate covers eight hours of work, so if you work longer than that, you'll be paid overtime. In addition to the session fee, you'll be paid for the use of the spot. The amount of these residuals vary depending on what networks the spot runs, how often it runs and for how long it runs. The more people exposed to the spot, the higher the residual payments. I'll give you an idea of how much these payments can be in Chapter 10, but you should know that residuals are invaluable to some actors, and can be substantial. They rely on them to bridge the money gap between jobs.

The SAG/AFTRA commercials contract also stipulates a session fee to be paid for each spot you do. So if you do five spots, you'll get five session payments, even if you shoot all of them in one day. And of course you'll get five residual payments for those spots as they air.

Remember that the producers can use the spot for a specific length of time. In TV, that period is 13 weeks, after which they have to renew that license. They do this by paying what's called a holding fee, which is equal to the amount of a scale session fee. By paying this fee, the client is saying that they don't want you to take any work from any of their competitors. They don't want you to pitch their product and a similar product at the same time. If you did a spot for Ford, a holding fee means you can't do a spot for Chevy while Ford's holding your spot. If you did, that's called a product conflict, and you'd be in a lot of trouble. In fact, if Ford found out about your Chevy spot, they'd ask you to pay back the money they gave you to not work for Chevy, or any other car company. And if Chevy found out that you had a Ford spot running, they'd make you pay back the money *they* paid you to not work for another car company. It makes more sense to avoid auditions for a competing product when you're getting holding fees. Your session payment acts as your first holding fee, so for the first thirteen weeks you definitely can't work for a competitor. If Ford pays you another holding fee at the end of the first thirteen weeks, they're holding the spot for another round. Until Ford stops paying holding fees, you can't work for another car company. This only applies to TV spots, whether you did on camera or VO. There's no conflict in radio.

The unions' contracts limit the amount of time a company can hold you for a spot and keep your product conflict in force. It's called a maximum period of use, and it's 21 months from the day you did the job. If Ford holds your spot that whole time, they've paid you holding fees every thirteen weeks. But if they want to continue holding the spot past that date, they can only do so with your permission. No actor ever gives their permission without a raise, so your agent calls Ford's ad agency and tells them you'd be happy to let them continue holding the spot if they pay you more money. Typically agents are able to get a 25% raise, which means that every check you get for that spot will be 25% greater than those you were receiving. Sweet, huh? A new date for a maximum period of use will be put into effect, and you'll be paid your new rate the whole time until they release the spot or the second use period ends. If it ends and they want to keep holding the spot, you'll get another raise. The downside to this is that you're still unable to work for any of Ford's competitors while you're getting holding fees, but hey, you're making money for not working, so you can't really complain.

You might think this is a little strange, that one company can dictate for whom else you work, but remember, you're getting paid *not* to work. And the beauty part is that you get a holding fee for every spot you do. If you do five Ford spots, you get five holding fees every thirteen weeks, in addition to five residual checks. The money adds up.

Speaking of money adding up, the unions also have made sure actors are covered if their spot winds up on the Internet. SAG rules say that you must be paid multiple session fees per spot if it is to run online for a year. All together now: Cha-ching!

If you think about it, the residual system is all about protecting the actor's image. As an actor, your face is really all you have. Residuals not only compensate you for helping to market a company's wares, but also to discourage them from using your image too much, thereby limiting your future employment potential. This is another essential goal of the union, and one of the main reasons why actors want to join.

Other Perks

The union contracts have several other benefits built into them. For example, if you do an AFTRA job, your agent's commission is paid by the producer, not by you. So if you're owed $1000, you'll get the entire amount, instead of kicking $100 to your agent. However, if you do a SAG job, this isn't the case, and your agent's commission comes out of your earnings.

Other perks for actors include a fee for wardrobe use. If you bring wardrobe to a job and you wear it for the shoot, you get $19 for your trouble, more if you brought formal wear. The producer also incurs a fee if you're made to work longer than six hours without a lunch break. It's called a meal penalty, and it's there to discourage producers from working you too long without a break. If for some reason you're booked on a job, and it gets canceled within 24 hours of your call time, you'll still be paid in full.

Not long ago I auditioned for an on camera narration job for a cola manufacturer. My agent called at 10:00 in the morning and told me that I was booked the next day. She called back at 2:00 to let me know that they had decided to go with someone else. Turns out they wanted to cast an actor who was older than me. While I was disappointed, it was still fine by me – they canceled less than 24 hours from my call time, so I got paid for working a whole day, even though I was at home washing my car.

Finally, the contracts say that actors must be paid within 30 days of doing a job. If you're not, the producer has to pay you a late fee. I've been paid in as little as two weeks.

Union actors also enjoy many other perks including discounts on wireless phone plans, access to the union's own credit union, panel discussions, meet-and-greets with agents and casting directors, discounts on loans and other financial products, and of course free DVDs of movies nominated for best picture in the Screen Actors Guild awards. Yes, as a member of SAG, you get to vote and help decide who wins a SAG award. Pretty cool.

Union Benefits

As a union member you have access to health insurance and retirement plans, which is pretty important these days. The producers pay much of the cost to run these plans. When they pay you for your services, they pay an additional fee to the union that amounts to about 15% of whatever you're paid for doing the job. This goes for both on camera and voice over work. So if you're paid $1000, the producer pays about $150 on top of that to help defray the cost of quality health and retirement plans. Actors have to qualify for these plans by earning enough money in any given year. That makes sense, because you have to pull your weight. In other words, the higher your earnings, the more they help fund the plans. If you don't work much, your earnings don't really contribute, so the union doesn't let you enroll. Once you qualify for the health plan, you can decide whether or not to participate, and if you do, you'll have to pay a very reasonable quarterly premium. You're automatically enrolled in the retirement plan once you earn enough to qualify for it. You can find the current minimum qualification levels on the unions' web sites. Currently AFTRA requires you to earn at least $10,000 in a year for health coverage, and SAG is closer to $15,000.

I can't stress enough how important it is to have access to affordable health insurance. If you're going to make acting your full time job, you're considered to be an independent contractor employed by many companies for a very short period of time. None of these companies will offer you benefits, and for self-employed workers, affordable health insurance is very hard to find. When we do find it on our own, the coverage might be sketchy at best. The unions' health plans are terrific, and are very affordable. The downside is that they're not open to every member, only those who qualify for them by booking enough union work. It's possible that you may have health coverage one year, but lose it the next because you didn't work as much. That is still better than paying for individual health coverage in the open market every year, which could cost a fortune.

These perks, however, don't come free. In addition to paying hefty fees to join, union members pay dues twice a year. The amount is based upon your earnings in the previous year and increase as you earn more money. Dues for SAG currently begin at $116 plus 1.85% of all your SAG earnings and rise from there. AFTRA's base dues are currently $63.90 plus 0.743% of your earnings, and increase as you make more money. Both unions cap an actor's dues somewhere north of $2,000, which personally I don't understand. If you're paying that much in dues, you're clearly making a ton of cash and you can probably afford to pay a lot more. But what do I know? I just work here.

Life As A Nonunion Actor

Working as a nonunion actor is a great way to learn the ins and outs of the business here in Chicago. Producers of nonunion projects are much more accepting of actors with less experience than they are in the union world. The nonunion world has its challenges and perks, but more than anything else it's a great place to get an education. I worked for years as a nonunion actor, and learned a lot about the business from people who wanted me to do well.

The work available is much the same as in the union world. Actors are needed for spots, industrials and voice over work. Nonunion agents get called for print and trade show work as well. There's also promotional work, which is a general term for a wide variety of jobs like handing out samples of perfume in department stores or working a company-sponsored event on a golf course. These are jobs where you're not necessarily acting, but you're still required to be professional. I was once asked to spend a day walking up and down Michigan Avenue while wearing a sandwich board handing out product samples. I respectfully declined.

Nonunion Opportunities

The vast majority of work that nonunion actors do is on camera industrials, spots and voice over, but you won't be doing exactly the same work as your union counterparts. As a general rule the clientele nonunion actors work for will not be the large advertising agencies in town. This means that you won't have a chance to work for brands like McDonald's, Ford, AT&T or The Home Depot. That's because those agencies have agreements with the unions that require them to use union talent for their client's commercials. They won't be looking in the nonunion world to cast their spots, so if you've always wanted to pitch Kraft cheese, you're out of luck. You might do an industrial for one of these companies, but not a commercial.

Another big difference between the union and nonunion world is that there's no residual system in place and no holding fees. I was shocked to learn this when I first started out. I had heard about residuals and I asked my voice over teacher about the subject. After explaining the basics he finished by saying, "This doesn't apply unless you're in the union." I was caught off guard. I thought all actors were entitled to residuals. Not so. All nonunion work is paid on a fee-for-service basis. You get paid for your time on the job, and that's all. The producer owns the final product and can use it however they want, and for however long they want, without paying you anything else unless a use fee has been negotiated.

There are many stories about talent shooting or recording a project that airs for years, even decades, without further payment. The most shocking story I've heard is one told by Richard Schoen, an actor and voice talent who was, way back at the beginning of his studio career when he sang non-union sessions, booked to sing on the "Save Big Money At Menards" campaign. The chain of home centers is still using the song today on TV, radio and in all their stores almost 30 years later. They have lifted his performance many hundreds of times, each time creating a new commercial; and they have counted on his voice for nearly three decades to help build the Menards brand. He was paid $250 for his work. On the flip side, I know an actor who did a spot which ran for over 20 years. It was a union spot, so he was paid every 13 weeks that entire time. Makes sense to me, because the company sold a lot of stuff during that time thanks to that spot, so it's good that he was being rewarded for helping out.

In recent years, nonunion agents have taken a cue from the unions and try to negotiate usage fees for their talent. These fees are called buyouts, and they usually cover one or two years worth of use. So the actor gets a certain amount for the session and a buyout for the usage. Technically and legally, there are no product conflicts in the nonunion world because no holding fees are being paid. That said, consider this scenario: Bill, a nonunion actor, does a bunch of TV spots for a small beer company. His agent negotiates a two-year deal that will pay him for both the session and use. He knows those spots could air anywhere for at least the next two years, maybe more if the company decides to renew the deal. Bill's got aspirations to join the unions, so he's with an agent that regularly sends him on union auditions. About six months after the beer spots start running, an audition for Bud Light comes up. Being perfect for it, Bill sails through the audition process and gets the job. In the interest of full disclosure, Bill's agent lets the clients know that he's got other beer spots running. Bud Light decides to go with another actor, one that's not currently pitching a competing product.

This makes sense. Why would Bud Light, a major national advertiser, hang the success of their brand on someone who's on air selling some other beer? They shouldn't and they don't.

I know what you're thinking: Bill's agent could have kept that information to herself. True, but these things always come out. All it takes is someone from Bud's ad agency seeing Bill in the other spots, and the pain begins. Bud could make him pay back all the money he got from doing their spots. On top of that, once word of what happened gets around it's unlikely that he'd be called in by Chicago's casting directors. By trying to do too much, Bill and his agent just put a huge dent in his career.

Nonunion actors have to think about conflicts, even though there aren't any in the official sense like there is in the union world. If you're hoping to have a crack at Chicago's big commercial jobs, you'll have to decide whether to take or skip some nonunion work. When I was nonunion I took whatever came my way, but I also knew that came with some risk. I was never in a Bill's position, but many actors will find themselves losing work because of their past choices.

In case you're wondering, here's a very short list of big advertisers that cast in Chicago:

Ford, Pillsbury, Gatorade, Sprint, Kraft, Proctor & Gamble, AT&T, Verizon, Home Depot, Miller, Budweiser, SC Johnson, Kellogg's, Comcast, United Airlines, Bissell, Nike, Quaker Oatmeal, Sears, Subway, H&R Block, McDonald's, Bob Evans, Best Buy, General Motors, and Volkswagen.

Independence

When you're a nonunion actor, you're on your own in the sense that there's no one watching over the producer's actions except you and your agent. You could shoot an industrial and after the final edit the producer could cut your footage into another video and a TV spot. If they don't tell you about the two other projects, there would be no way for you to know unless you saw them somewhere. This means that you really shot three projects and only got paid for one. If they had told your agent about the additional projects upfront, the agent would have negotiated a fee for all of them. Instead, you're out of luck, and there's nothing you or your agent can do besides make a phone call to try to get more money. But the client can say no, and that's pretty much the end of it. There are strict rules in place governing lifted footage that must be followed by producers hiring union talent. The rules say that actors must be paid for any project which features their voice or likeness. In the nonunion world, there are no such rules. It's up to you to go after anything that's used for a purpose other than what you agreed to when you did the job.

I don't want to give the impression that producers who hire non-union talent are dishonest. The vast majority of them are great folks, but there are bad apples in both the union and nonunion world. The difference is, in the union world you've got people backing you up. Remember my job where I slept on the couch all day? They lifted footage from that spot and turned it into a print ad, so the agency called my agent to ask how much they should pay for that use. My agent quoted them a price, and I was sent a check within a month. If they hadn't called and I found out about the print ad, the agency would have faced fines from the union. If they decided that they didn't want to pay the fines, the union would take them to court to get the fees. That would cost them even more in attorney's fees. So ultimately, union producers follow the rules because it makes more financial sense than to try and get out of paying actors. Nonunion producers can take the chance that an actor's not going to find out about a lift because there's little financial risk involved.

Nonunion actors are as protected as their agents can make them. Agents tell producers to pay talent within thirty days of the job, and many do; but those who don't can hold off because there's really no consequence. Your agent will send them overdue invoices, but that's about it. If the producer doesn't pay you at all, the agent can threaten to take them to court. But you can bet that won't happen unless the job is worth a ton of money. If you're owed $300 for a voiceover job, it'll cost that much to file a law suit. You're probably just going to get stiffed.

There are a few other protections that you won't have access to as a nonunion actor. There's no wardrobe fee in the nonunion world, nor is there a meal penalty. Overtime is usually paid, but sometimes it isn't, and you'll be told when you're walking into a job that could last for 18 hours. Also, if you're a nonunion actor you don't have access to health or retirement benefits from your acting work. You'll need to have another job that provides you with insurance, or you'll have to buy it on your own. The good news is that most nonunion agents have a cancellation fee in place so you're compensated for holding time open for a job.

I know a lot of this sounded like a bunch of gloom and doom, like I'm against the idea of being a nonunion actor. That's not the case at all. It was hugely beneficial for me for a long time, and I learned a lot working with a bunch of great people. Most of the jobs you'll do will pay well and you'll be paid in a reasonable amount of time. Most of the people you work with will be friendly professionals who want you to have a good experience working for them, but I also want to be straight with you about what to expect when you're a nonunion actor.

Making The Choice

So far, everything in this chapter has been based in fact. I've kept out my personal views, but from here on out, I'm going to give you my opinion. After all you bought this book to get some insight from someone who's been around the block a couple times.

At some point in their career, every professional actor has to make the decision about whether or not to join a union. It usually comes later for Chicago actors than it does for talent in Los Angeles or New York. Because the unions are so entrenched in those markets, there's less nonunion work being done there, so the choice is pretty simple. If you want to work in those cities, you have to be in the unions.

Here in Chicago, the picture isn't as clear. The unions have a large presence, but there's also a lot of nonunion work. This is especially true of industrials, and as time passes, is becoming truer for commercials. Some actors in Chicago have no intention of ever joining SAG or AFTRA; there's enough nonunion work to keep them busy without having to be a member of anything but a health club. So it's not as though union membership is a prerequisite to make a living as a Chicago actor, but my story might help you to decide what you want for your own career.

One Way To Go

No one is born with a union card in their hand. I started out just like most actors in Chicago, by working in the nonunion world. I didn't even know that the unions existed until about a year into my career. At some point, probably by talking to other actors, I figured out that there was this thing called a union and I wasn't in it. I realized I was working behind a kind of curtain and that there was work being done that I didn't have a shot at getting. That bothered me. I was in the business to make a living. If there was a whole segment of it I couldn't take part in, I had to do whatever it took to gain access to it. I wanted to find a way to see behind the curtain.

I started getting as much information about the unions as I could. This was when the Internet was in its infancy, and most websites were glorified billboards with little information. Luckily, I landed in classes that were taught by union actors, and I asked lots of questions. Over time I put together a picture of what I was missing out on, and it was quite a lot.

I started paying attention to the kind of opportunities I had as a nonunion actor. At first I didn't care who I worked for so long as they paid me, but after a while I started thinking that it might be cool if I did a job that had some zing to it – some panache. Something like a car commercial, where I'd be driving a convertible down a curvy road, the wind in my hair, a pretty girl by my side, or perhaps a cruise ship commercial, where I'd be snorkeling and playing beach volleyball during the day and winning jackpots in the casino at night. Instead, I was selling aluminum siding, or talking about cheese. These jobs paid the bills, but I was bored.

I started wondering why I never got to audition for any cool jobs like those car spots, and I started asking around. I went to my teachers with the question, and they explained that those kinds of projects were open only to union members. After thinking about it, I figured that all the jobs I wanted access to were union. If I wanted to do big national commercials, I'd have to be in the union. If I wanted to do movies or TV, I had to join the union. If I wanted the opportunity to make money for doing nothing, I wasn't going to get it by being nonunion. I came to the realization that joining SAG and AFTRA was the only way to keep my career moving onward and upward.

But there was a catch. I found out that once you go union, you can't go back. When you join a union, you agree to follow Rule One, which is that you don't do nonunion work. The benefits that come with being in a union like collective bargaining, residuals, health insurance and the rules written to protect actors come at a price. The union asks for your loyalty in return. If you make yourself available as a nonunion actor, you're working against the concept of being in a union, and if enough actors did that, the unions would up and disappear. Besides, why would a producer hire you through the union if you're available for less money as a nonunion actor? That would render your status as a union member totally useless. This made sense to me, but I was nervous to say goodbye to all the work that I had become accustomed to getting. It took a little while for me to reach a point where I was willing to make the jump.

While I was considering what I wanted, I started noticing something else besides the fact that I couldn't audition for cool projects. The nonunion world is filled with very professional people on both sides of the camera, but it also has a higher percentage of people who are less so. Don't send me nasty emails about this. I'm not saying that actors and producers on nonunion jobs are lousy. But since most new actors are nonunion and they have less experience, they're less professional than someone who knows their way around a set. Working with them can be a challenge. Also, when producers start their career, they're more likely to land at production companies that do a lot of nonunion work. This means that there are a higher percentage of producers and directors in the nonunion world who have yet to develop a professional way of working. Also, companies who frequently run on very tight budgets are not going to hire a union actor. They'll try to get nonunion actors for the lowest possible price. The nonunion world is also home to companies who rarely hire actors, meaning they don't have any idea what actors do and thus have no respect for their time or talent. The hassle factor in the nonunion world is higher than it is in the union world.

I began to discover this as I worked for more and more nonunion producers. I had mostly great experiences, but the lousy ones began to add up. I had to chase down money. I had to deal with weird requests, like the director who didn't want me to use my EAR on a job with an ungodly amount of material. He was new and someone told him that actors who used the EAR would take too much time on the set and drag the job out, a notion which couldn't be further from the truth. I had to deal with agents who worked more for their client than they did for me because they were afraid of losing their client. They were never afraid of losing me. At some point I began noticing how much of my time was spent dealing with hassles instead of just doing my job. It was turning out that I wasted a lot of time and energy dealing with stuff that I shouldn't have had to deal with in the first place. The low point came when I found myself threatening to sue an agent who wasn't paying me for a job, even after presenting them with evidence from the client that the invoice had been paid. That did it. I was done. I made the decision to grab the next chance I had to join the unions.

I don't want to give you the idea that the nonunion world is rife with unscrupulous, dishonest bums who don't know which end of a camera to point towards an actor. It's quite the opposite. Like I said, I learned a great deal from being a nonunion actor because I was fortunate enough to work with some people who were very good at their jobs. But possibly the most important thing I learned during that time was this: If you're a professional actor you have to manage your career, or it will manage you.

Be ProACTive

You can't rely on things just happening. You have to take action to make them happen. If you want to work in voice over, you can't assume your agents will read your mind and submit you for that work. You have to tell them you want it, and you have to train to be able to do it. Likewise, if you want to be considered for film and TV, you have to be out there working in the theater. If you don't, you'll spend a lot of time wondering why you don't get those auditions. Going with the flow and letting things happen is a good way to become frustrated when the things you *hope* will happen, aren't.

For any actor who relies on the industry for a full time income, it's not enough to sit back and take whatever work comes your way. Do that and you'll never realize your full potential. Instead, you have to consciously make decisions about where you want to go. This is never truer than when you're faced with the prospect of joining one of the unions. Actors who spend time in the nonunion world will eventually have to decide if they're happy there or not. Some will be, but others won't. If you find yourself in the second group, you'll have to decide how you feel about giving up working with some of the agents and producers you have relationships with. There are agents in Chicago who go after both union and nonunion work and if you're with one of them, you can stay there after you become union. However a few agents only do nonunion work, and you'll have to leave them if you want to be in SAG or AFTRA. Same thing goes for producers.

This means sacrificing in the short term for a long term gain. The question is: will union membership be worth the short term sacrifice? For me, the answer was a resounding yes, but it didn't happen overnight. The year I joined the unions was difficult for a number of reasons. On the agent front, I was fortunate because I was listed with several of them who did both kinds of work, but I did have to leave the agent that brought me the *most* work. That was psychologically difficult to do, especially since it took so long to develop that relationship. It also wound up being financially hard because my income took a pretty good dip that year. This was because most producers I had worked for in the past only hired nonunion actors, and many of them booked me without an audition. Without them, I lost all of that repeat business. I could earn only what I made from new work, which was harder to come by now that I was auditioning exclusively against union actors. I was now a small fish in a bigger, more competitive pond.

Competition

It's harder to book a union job than it is to book a nonunion one. That's because most union actors have fine-tuned what they do. Auditioning against them is tough, because the competition is fierce. That doesn't mean that actors are tripping each other in the waiting room, but everyone is there to book the job, and they all know how to do it. When you audition against a bunch of union actors, you'd better bring your "A" game every time, because you'll be up against a ton of people who do a terrific audition. This is less true in a nonunion audition. In those auditions you might be going up against 20 or 30 people, and they'll all have varying levels of experience. Some will be very experienced, others less so. That means there will be fewer quality auditions. The seasoned actors will be compared only to those actors with the same level of ability. If 30 people audition and only fifteen are experienced, the producer will consider only the 15 solid auditions, automatically increasing the chances of the actors who did well. On the other hand, auditioning in a group of thirty union actors means the producer will probably see thirty solid auditions.

When I was new to the union, it took me a while to learn how to do well in the face of this kind of competition. I was used to the numbers working for me as I learned how to audition really well, but when I jumped to the union side I discovered that everyone else had learned those skills too. Now I was up against a greater number of good actors every time I auditioned for work, especially if the audition was at a casting director's office. Eventually though, I found my footing and started landing work.

My transition from nonunion to union did not happen by itself. It only happened because I made the decision to move in that direction. Union membership seemed to match up with the goals I had set for myself. So I saw it as just another logical step in my career, like getting into on camera work after starting out as a voice talent. I didn't make this decision lightly. I looked at it from a lot of different angles and compared notes with other actors. I picked the brains of my agents and teachers, as well. After thinking about it for a long time, I came to three realizations. First, the talks with my agents told me that I worked more than the average nonunion actor in my age group. I thought everyone worked as much as I did, but most didn't. That gave me the feeling that since I was doing well as a nonunion actor, I should be able to work in the union world. Secondly, I realized that by staying nonunion I would be putting a ceiling on my income because I could only do one job at a time. The union pay structure allowed actors to make money without physically being on the job. Lastly, I wanted to be able to work without the hassles that I was running into, or at least without having to deal with them as much. These three things all added up to my decision to take the risk and go union. Looking back, it was a great decision to make.

Now It's Your Turn

So what about you? How should you manage your career? Obviously I can't answer that for you, but here's what I think. If your acting is a part time endeavor, then don't worry about the unions. There's enough nonunion work out there to keep you busy. Acting can be a fantastic part time job. The work you'll get will pay way better than ones you'll find in retail or in restaurants. Book a commercial or two, a few good industrials and a trade show and you've made as much or more than if you worked twenty hours a week all year long in those other jobs. If that's as far as you want your acting career to take you, being nonunion is fine.

If you want to act for a living, it's my opinion that being nonunion isn't enough. I'm talking to the people who believe acting is their calling – the people who can't imagine themselves doing anything other than acting. If you plan on being an actor for a very long time, and you plan on it providing a single source of income for your family, you must get yourself into the unions eventually. You don't have to join right away. In fact, I think you should stay nonunion for as long as you can. It's the perfect way to learn the business, hone your skills and get you to the point where you're very comfortable working in a variety of areas. After you've got auditioning down, you're consistently being called back and you're booking a lot of jobs, working nonunion may get to be stale for you. You might be the big fish in the nonunion pond, but you'll always wonder what it would be like to book a national union spot or work on a big time film. Add to that the fact that you might be waiting too long to get paid for the work you do. If you're like me, you'll naturally start to think about what's next for you, and that could be going after union membership. Actors like us will always want to see what's on the other side of the curtain. And if we don't, it'll eat at us until we pull it aside and have a peek.

Here's another big reason why you should consider union membership: there's nothing in the nonunion world for you once you reach a certain level. Once you've become the go-to person for the kind of work you do well, what are you going to do? You'll do the same thing over and over again for the same amount of money. If you're hoping that one day you'll be hired by a company who'll want you to do all their spots, industrials and print work, that day might well come. But they'll try to get you for so little it may not be worth it. There is such a thing as being overexposed. That means you're so often seen pitching a company's product that the public starts to identify you with that product, and that product only. If that happens long enough, no one else will hire you again for a long time. Suddenly the money you made won't seem like a lot when you can't get another job. When that happens in the union world actors don't care much because they've walked away with millions. Do you think you'll ever see the Verizon guy again after they retire him from their campaign? No way. Not unless he changes his look to the point that he's unrecognizable. The character he plays has been so ingrained in the nation's consciousness as the promoter of Verizon's service, that he will forever be that guy to us. But it doesn't really matter because he's already a very wealthy actor thanks to the union contracts. If he did all that work as a nonunion actor, he'd be doing well as long as he was working, but he wouldn't retire a millionaire. Not even close. When the campaign came to an end, he'd have to start working when his money ran out, and he'd find a difficult road.

If you're like me, and you like to see your career steadily move onward and upward, you're better off using the nonunion world as a proving ground. Count on it as a place to learn, compete and refine your ability. Then, when you're ready, move on to union membership and much greater earning potential.

Remember though, timing is everything. There are as many stories floating around about actors who join the union too soon as there are about actors who have nonunion spots run for years without additional compensation. Some actors get lucky very early in their career. They land a union commercial, become Taft-Hartley, and wind up doing a second or third spot for that client after their thirty days have expired. So they join the union before they've done much else. Then, when the advertiser no longer needs them, they don't work again for a very long time. While they were perfect for those few spots, they aren't competitive in other auditions because they haven't yet developed their skills. They find themselves auditioning against professionals who are much better prepared, and they don't do as well.

You shouldn't join the unions until you're ready. You'll know when you are because you'll get feedback from teachers, agents and producers. A big hint is when directors ask why you aren't union. I had several ask me that question, and it helped me to realize that I was missing out on something. If the people who hire you don't understand why you're doing their nonunion job, you should be giving serious thought to going union.

How Low Can You Go?

There's one last point I want to make about union vs. nonunion. This business is cyclical whether you're in a union or not. It rises and falls with the economy. If companies are spending money, there's plenty of work for Chicago actors. If not, there's a lot less work to go around. One final protection you'll have if you're a union member is the fact that no matter how slow the economy gets, producers won't try to lower your rates. They can't. They're bound by the contracts to hire you at scale. The worst that could happen is that if you're used to working for rates that are over scale, you'll be asked to bring them down to scale. This is in contrast to the nonunion producers who can pay actors whatever they think they can get them for. During our recent recession, nonunion actors reported rates falling by as much as 40%. Actors were doing the same work as before the recession, but companies were cutting budgets, reducing spending, or just using the economic climate to get talent for less. Agents did what they could to keep the fees up, but ultimately the issue is in the hands of the actors, who have two unpalatable choices: work for less money or say no, and know the job will go to someone else. That's one of the problems with the nonunion world. There will always be someone else to take work no matter how little it pays. If enough people agree to take pay cuts, the lower rates will become the norm, and it'll be tough to bring them back up when the economy turns around. Just something to think about.

Wrap Up

Everything I've written about thus far has been for actors who follow the typical path in Chicago, meaning nonunion to union. There are, however, actors who go the other way. They join the union and find that they're not booking the amount of work they thought they would for a variety of reasons. Work trends shift to other cities, life gets in the way and career plans change. If an actor decides to step away from their membership, the unions have a process for that. You can find out more about suspending your member status by visiting each union's website.

The bottom line is that if you want to be in the running for the work that's exciting to do and that pays well, you'll have to be in the union. Since I brought up the topic of money, let's talk about that next.

CHAPTER TEN

Your Income From Acting In Chicago

Have you jumped to this chapter without reading any of the previous ones? I don't blame you. We're talking about making a living as an actor and you need to know how much you can make. But if you haven't read anything up to this point, do yourself a favor and read the chapter on unions. If you're familiar with them, this chapter will be easier to understand. I'd prefer you read the entire book from start to finish, but do whatever works for you.

I'm going to get very specific about how much money actors can earn; but before I do there are some things I feel obligated to say. I hope you're not getting into this career for the money, because if you are, I promise that there are better industries to explore. Trade stocks. Invent a product everyone needs. Write some indispensable bit of software. These careers are almost definitely going to make you more money. Don't get me wrong, you can make a boatload as an actor, but the money should come as a complement to the main attraction, which is your love of acting and all it allows you to do.

Like everything else in this business, there's a ton of variation in the amount of money that any one actor can make. Many, many factors determine an actor's income level: how well the nation's economy is performing, whether or not an actor is union or nonunion, what kind of work the actor books, what "type" the actor is, whether the actor is full time or part time, which agent (or agents) the actor is with, how long the actor has been in the business, and the actor's training level. You get the picture.

There's a lot of uncertainty in every actor's career because you never know what's around the corner. Your next job could pay your mortgage for a year, or it could be a year until you see your next job. This aspect of the business applies to famous actors as well as the rank-and-file. It's hard to talk about averages, since even accomplished talent can experience dramatic swings in income from year to year. Sharon Wottrich, founder of Voices Unlimited (now Innovative Artists Chicago), used to tell stories about voice talent whose annual incomes rocketed to $750,000 virtually overnight and then crashed down to $250,000. These are extreme examples, but they illustrate the unpredictability of acting for a living. And I know what you're thinking, "If I made $250,000, I'd be pretty happy!" Me too, but if you lived a $750,000 lifestyle, a mere quarter million would seem pretty low. It's all relative.

I can't tell you how much an average Chicago actor makes in a year, though I'm sure it isn't north of two hundred grand. Any number would be inaccurate and give you a false sense of what to expect. Although there are actors in town who earn a million dollars in a year, there are also actors who are lucky to make a thousand.

So...What Can I Tell You?

There are three notions about money for the average Chicago actor that are true most of the time. How's that for definitive? Notion number one is the more experience you have, the more money you make. This makes sense, since newbies tend to learn on the job. It took me years to be able to book rates that were over scale, and I can only do that now because my experience helps me to stand out among the competition. I did a lot of learning by doing. However, there are also stories of new actors doing quite well without practicing much. They figured it out without having to put in much effort. Kudos to them.

Notion number two is that you make more money if you're union. This also makes sense since producers go with nonunion talent to save money. Traditionally nonunion rates are lower than union ones, so it stands to reason that union talent will make more per job. If two actors, one SAG/AFTRA and one not, do the same number of spots and industrials in a year you can expect the union talent to make more money. Unless the nonunion actor made tons of money in buyouts and overtime, the union actor should win the money race pretty easily thanks to the union's higher rates and residual system, but it really depends on how much work each actor books. If the nonunion actor does fifty jobs and the union actor does five, Mr. Nonunion is probably going to come out ahead unless Mr. Union's income is made up of high-dollar residuals, either from those jobs or ones from previous years. He physically worked less, but could possibly make more. So it just depends on the kind of work you do.

Notion number three is that you make more money if you're between the ages of 30 and 50. As a general rule, most of the commercials and industrials produced in Chicago are written for people in this age range. A ton of commercials feature moms and dads. A ton of industrials feature employees and managers. These people are likely to be in their 30s or 40s. A ton of voice over work calls for voices in this age range, too. Same goes for print and trade shows. This is not to say that there isn't work for folks who are outside of this age range, but there's more for those in it.

When I was in my mid-20s, one of my agents said she couldn't wait until I turned 30. Although I was doing well, she thought my career would really take off once I looked like I could be a dad. She was right. I aged into that work by my 31st birthday, and my career changed. I started booking more work simply because more was available to me. There's anecdotal evidence suggesting that on camera work is harder to come by for actors older than 50. This seems less true for voice talent since many of them stay busy well beyond that age. But if you've learned anything from this book, it's that there aren't any hard and fast rules. Your career could very well buck this trend. There's just no way to say for sure how busy you'll be no matter what age range you're in.

Strap Yourself In

There's a lot of money to be made in the Chicago market. Literally every day, multiple jobs are being worked on in all areas of the business. Most of these jobs pay very well. When I was starting out, my Mom used to ask how much I made per hour. She knew that sometimes I was on a job for only a short time, and when you did the math you got some crazy hourly wages. If I did a VO narration job for $300 and it took me an hour and a half, I made about $200 an hour! She used to get a kick out of how high my pay grade could be, and was amazed that I made what she called "lawyers' fees," for doing nothing more than talking out loud. That was fun to think about, but back then I didn't work that much. I reminded her that my jobs were few and far between. All actors try their hardest to make that kind of money all day every day!

As a professional actor your income will go up and down like a roller coaster, and short of getting another job there's little you can do to smooth out the bumpy ride. You could go from having your worst year to having your best year ever. It works the other way around, too. I've seen my income slashed by thirty percent only to have it double the next year.

What's amazing is that one client can make the difference between starving and ordering the steak. When I was the spokesperson for a cellular phone company, they accounted for a quarter of my income. I was nonunion then, and I was working in all areas of the business just like

I've always done. This company kept me pretty busy. They had me doing TV, radio and print. I worked for other companies during that time, but without the big client, I would have had a drastically different lifestyle. If you're a union actor, that one good relationship can make an even bigger difference. For a time, I was one of the online voices of a luxury car brand. I narrated multiple product videos for their website. They decided to lift portions of the audio for TV spots. Because of the union's residual system, that client accounted for 30 percent of my total income for that year.

That's not all that unusual. Actors everywhere, not just in Chicago, count on having one or two clients that bring in the big bucks for them. When the money comes in, it's smart to use it since you don't know when it'll come again. One year, Ford remodeled my kitchen. Another year, Motorola built a two-car garage for me. More recently, Hartford Insurance bought my wife's engagement ring.

Enough About Me – What Can You Make?

Let's get specific. You've learned that there are seven ways Chicago actors make money in the business besides working in theater. As we talk about exactly how much you can make in each of them, keep in mind your own situation. If you're new to the business, think about where you might want to focus your training so that you can get your share of the pie. If you have an existing career, look for ways to augment your earning power. What skill set do you think you might be able to develop that would result in the biggest financial gain? The more you can do, the more money you'll make.

Commercials

Actors all across the country count on commercials for at least a portion of their income. Union actors depend on the residuals to smooth out a bumpy income stream. Nonunion actors cite them as a reason they can avoid supplementing their acting income. The earning potential is much higher for union talent, but nonunion actors can still make a pretty good buck for a day's work.

Union Commercials

If you're a member of SAG or AFTRA, you can count on a nice chunk of money from a TV commercial, even if you're just paid scale. The fees change every three years as new contracts are negotiated, but currently a fee of $592.20 is paid for the shoot day, per spot. This is called a session fee. You'll also get something called a holding fee (unless the spot is made for cable only) every 13 weeks for as long as the advertiser wants the right to air the spot. This "holds" you for this advertiser in the sense that it prevents you from doing spots for competing products while you're in their ad. It's also $592.20 per spot. If you shoot more than one spot, or if the footage from your spot is used in multiple commercials, you'll get a holding fee for each one. Three spots equal three holding fees, five spots equal five holding fees, and so on.

In addition to session and holding fees, union members also get fees called residuals. This is money that advertisers pay for the right to air the spots you're in multiple times. Residuals are paid on a sliding scale, and vary widely depending on how often the spot runs, where it runs and for how long it runs. Generally, the more people that see it, the higher the residuals. There are national spots, regional spots and local spots. There are also spots that run on network, which means ABC, NBC, CBS and Fox, and cable, meaning the national cable networks like CNN and AMC. Advertisers sometimes shoot spots for specific dates. Car companies do this because their sales promotions tend to last for a short time. Other companies produce spots that are intended to be aired for a long time, maybe a year or more. The longer your spot runs, the more money you'll make because the holding fees and residuals add up.

Warning: Math Alert! I'm going to use some simple calculations to give you an idea of how this works. The math is pretty simple, and it'll be interesting for you to see how your earnings are calculated when you work in a union TV spot.

Here's An Example

Say you're a SAG scale performer (meaning your rates are not over scale) and you book one 30-second spot for Target, a big national retailer. Target is based in Minnesota. Since you're in Chicago, they fly you to Minneapolis for the job. You arrive the day before the shoot. You'll be paid $592.20 for the travel day. It's a one-day shoot, and it goes an hour into overtime. You'll make $592.20 for the shoot day, plus $74.00 for the overtime, bringing your total for the session to $1258.40. That's pretty nice for working one day, I think.

So that's your session fee, but what about residuals? These fees are calculated using a complicated formula based on a number of factors. Personally, I think it's only slightly less confusing than our income tax code. Here are a few things that determine how much you'll get paid: which cities the spot runs in, how many times the advertiser airs the spot, how long the spot is, whether it's aired on cable, network or both, whether it's made for cable only and if it is played on cable, how many subscribers the cable system has. It's impossible for me to explain all the variations that can change the numbers used to figure your paycheck. If you want to get an idea of them you can visit SAG's website. They have a chart that will explain the details and you can do all the arithmetic you want. For our hypothetical Target spot, I'm going to keep it fairly simple.

Let's say Target chooses to air your spot nationally on network. They have a couple of ways to handle the media buy. One option is to use a method that pays you for each time the spot runs. Advertisers like to do this when they know they're going to air the spot just a few times. In cases like these, they sometimes follow the Class A residual chart, which looks like this:

$$1^{st} \text{ use: } \$592.20$$
$$2^{nd} \text{ use: } \$135.80$$
$$3^{rd} \text{ use: } \$107.75$$
$$4^{th}\text{-}13^{th} \text{ use: } \$107.75 \text{ each}$$
$$14^{th} \text{ and above: } \$51.65 \text{ each}$$

If they air your spot 50 times using this chart, this is how the math works:

$$592.20 + 135.80 + 107.55 + 10(107.75) + 36(51.65) = \$3772.65$$

Pretty nice! When you add in the $1258.40 you got for your session, this Target job turns out to be a lucrative one. Before we figure the grand total, though, there's one last thing to consider. Your session fee of $592.20 also includes the payment for the first unit of use. Because of this rule your residual payment really totals $3180.45, instead of that final number above. Add that to your session fee of $1258.40, and you arrive at a grand total of $4438.85 for the session and network use. Not bad for working one day.

Paying actors Class A rates gets expensive, so there's another option advertisers use more frequently, and that's the wildspot buy. With a wildspot, your residual rates are determined based on where the spot runs instead of how many times it runs. As a wildspot, Target can run the spot an unlimited number of times in specific cities. Each city is scored based on population density, and that score is expressed in units. The higher a city's population, the higher the unit number. For example, St. Louis is three units, but Memphis is one unit. Dallas is seven units. The wildspot chart looks like this:

1st Unit: $592.20

Units 2-25: $20.27 each

Units 26-60: $7.52 each

Units 61-125: $7.52 each

Units 126 +$7.52 each

If Target wanted to air the spot just in St. Louis, Memphis and Dallas, the math would work out like this:

St. Louis = 3 units

Memphis = 1 unit

Dallas = 7 units

$$592.20 + 3(20.27) + 20.27 + 7(20.27) =$$

$$592.20 + 60.81 + 20.27 + 141.89 = \$815.17$$

Remember you've already been paid for your first unit in your session fee, so your final residual total is $815.17 minus $592.20, or $222.97. That's a whole lot less than using the Class A system, but Target gets the ad in front of a much smaller audience.

With wildspot buys, advertisers will often include one or more of the three major markets: Los Angeles, Chicago and New York. There are special rates for those cities, and the chart looks like this:

NYC alone: $1163.80

Chicago or L.A. alone: $1014.45

Two of three major markets NYC, Chicago, L.A.: $1601.60

All three major markets NYC, Chicago, L.A.: $1931.85

Each additional unit: $7.52

If Target wanted to air your spot in all three major markets plus St. Louis, Memphis and Dallas, the math would looks like this:

$$1931.85 + 3(20.27) + 20.27 + 7(20.27) =$$
$$1931.85 + 60.81 + 20.27 + 141.89 = \$2154.82$$

In this case I left the payment for the first unit out since it was already paid in the session fee. If you add $2154.82 to the $1258.40 you got for the session that brings the total for the session and network use to $3413.22. Again, it's not as much as you'd get if the spot ran 50 times on Class A rates, but Target hasn't gotten the ad in front of as many eyeballs, either.

These rates are all for network and don't include any airtime on cable stations. There are separate rate charts for cable, and if Target wants to hit a bunch of cable channels in addition to their network buy, they'll have to pay you for that use separately.

The concept of units is extended to the cable networks as well. This time it's not a measurement of population, but subscribers. The higher the number of subscribers, the higher the unit number. For example, CNN is 285 units, AMC is 274 units, and The Big Ten Network is 123 units. The SAG rates for cable look like this:

Minimum: $592.20
Units 1-50 = $9.95
Units 51-100 = $8.64
Units 101-150 = $7.34
Units 151-200 = $6.03
Units 201-1,000 = $0.71
Units 1001 – 2000 = $0.67
Maximum = $2836.00

Notice that there's a minimum and a maximum. If a spot is going to air on a cable channel, the least you'll make is a scale session fee, or $592.20, but the most you'll make is just over $2800.

Now, back to our example. Target's already paid you a good buck on the session and network use. If they want to get some cable exposure along with what they've already bought, they'll have to fork over some more cash. Let's say they want to cover the cable channels pretty well, and buy time on channels that total 1700 units. Following the rate chart above, they'll pay a total of $2635.00. Look:

$$50(9.95) + 50(8.64) + 50(7.34) + 50(6.03)$$
$$+ 800(.71) + 700(.67) = \$2635$$

If Target decides to post your spot online, you'll get an additional $787.63 for eight weeks of use. If they wanted it on the Internet for a year, you'll get an additional $2072.70.

So let's total everything up:

Session:	$1258.40
Network Wildspot Use:	$2154.82
Cable Use	$2635.00
Internet Use (8 weeks)	$787.63 +
Total	$6835.85

Two words: Cha ching! Remember, you were on the set for one day, and you made nearly $7000 for the time you were there. That's like $760 per hour!

Keep in mind that this is just a hypothetical situation. You could make more or less from that Target spot. As I said before, sometimes one becomes two spots or more, and you're paid for all of them. If your spot was cut into three spots, you'd be paid triple what you'd make for one. If you landed one job that paid you about $20,000 in one year that would be a jackpot.

Hold Off On The Shopping Spree

On the flip side, there's no guarantee that the spot will ever air. Plenty of commercials are made but never see the light of day. In that case you're paid for the session and that's all. What's worse is when you shoot a commercial and expect to get all the holding fees and residuals, but then discover that you were left on the cutting room floor. When this happens, it's called a downgrade, and it means that you were edited out. This can happen for a variety of reasons, but often occurs in spots where many actors were hired as principals. Think street scenes, bar scenes, and party scenes. The only bright side to this situation is that you'll get a downgrade fee equal to one session fee. But then the money stops. Thankfully this is pretty rare. When it does happen, it feels a bit like someone smacked you in the gut with a tire iron. Trust me, I know. It's happened to me.

But Wait There's More!

Advertisers pay other fees in addition to the ones you get. In our example, Target will also be contributing about 15% of what they're paying you toward your health and retirement benefits. You need to qualify for these benefits by working, and the Target job is valuable since it would start your year off in a nice way. Heck, it's possible that you'd get your health insurance from just that one booking.

Can Target run your spot forever? Technically yes, but they'll pay for the privilege. As mentioned previously, there's a time limit on how long the spot can run. It's called the "maximum period of use," and it's there to protect performers from being bound to the advertiser for life.

If you shoot the Target spot on February 1st of 2010, Target will have the right to air the spot for 21 consecutive months from the day of the shoot. After November 1st, 2011, they'll have to ask for your permission to renew it. Pretty cool. Even cooler is that your agent will only let you say "yes" if Target gives you a raise. Often it's 25%, but sometimes it's more. This means that your holding fees and residuals will be at least 25% more than they were before. Once they agree to pay you more, another 21-month period begins. If they want to renew a second time, you'll get another raise, and you'll continue to get holding fees and residuals until it's time to renew a third time, and on and on. You can see that eventually this will get pretty expensive for Target, and sooner or later they'll release the spot, which is what happens when they no longer want to air it. At this point the spot's life and the money you've been making from it will come to an end. This releases you from your obligation to them, and you'll be free to do commercials for their competitors.

Never-ending holding fees are great, but sometimes you don't want to be attached to a company. A few years back I did all the voice over work for a wireless carrier. It was a small one, nothing the size of Verizon or Sprint, but it was a nice gig for me. After about three years (which is a long time in this business), they had a change of heart. They decided to use someone else as their voice. As a farewell gift, they asked me to appear on camera in one spot. I was glad to have the job, but what I didn't know was how long they were going to hold it. They held that thing for a LONG time, way past the first 21 months ended, but they never aired it. I got holding fees, but no residuals. It was irritating because of the conflict rule. That one spot took me out of the running for doing any TV (VO or on camera) for any other wireless phone company. At the time, AT&T and Verizon did a lot of casting in Chicago, and I had to pass on those auditions, ones that would have led to far more money than I was making from the holding fees of this one, stinkin' little spot. It was bad enough that they replaced me as their voice, but then they pulled the band-aid off slowly over the course of almost three years. I about threw a party when the spot was released.

Sometimes you want your spots to be renewed until the cows come home. When you've done a spot for a furniture store, or a professional association, or a utility company, you hope and pray that they hold it forever. When a company has few competitors who advertise, that's good for actors in their spots. Why? Remember, you're bound to them for the duration of the spot. If there's not much advertising being done by businesses like theirs, you do the happy dance because you're getting paid AND you won't have to say "I can't do that," to agents that call you with juicy auditions. If you shoot a local spot for ComEd that means you won't be able to do one for their competitors. Oh wait, ComEd doesn't HAVE a competitor in Chicago. If you do a spot for the American Medical Association that means that you'll be in conflict with other medical associations. How many of those do you see putting ads on TV? The other side of that coin includes companies like automakers, beer brewers, insurance companies or retailers. There's a million of each, and they all advertise on TV. When you work for one, you'll be in conflict with the rest until your spot is released.

A Little Reality Check

The Target example was useful for you to see how the higher end of the union commercial spectrum works, but there are a lot of spots made that won't get that kind of airplay. I don't want you to come away thinking that every TV spot you shoot will make you $7000 every 13 weeks for years. Spots that run locally and regionally don't make that kind of money. I've made plenty of commercials that paid a session and a few hundred dollars worth of use. But I've also had spots earn a lot more than our example. It just depends on what kind of work you book.

Nonunion Commercials

How is all this different for nonunion performers? Money. Typical nonunion commercials pay between $250 and $500 per spot for the session. Nonunion agents try to get buyout fees in place of residuals, but they're not always successful. If they are, your buyout could double or triple what you made for the session. In exchange for the buyout, they can air the spot as often, and on as many networks as they want without paying you any additional money. So if your session was $500 and your buyout was $1500, your total earnings for that spot would be $2000. Again, not bad for a day's worth of work in front of a camera.

If your agent can't get a buyout, you'll earn a session fee and nothing more. Then the client can air the spot as long as they want without paying you anything else, ever again. Some spots air for years. In cases where this happens, agents will likely get in touch with the client to ask for more money, but the client is under no obligation to pay anything beyond your session fee unless the spot was negotiated to run for a limited time. There are no holding fees in the nonunion world, and no health and retirement contributions, either.

Free bargaining rules the nonunion roost. That means you and your agent (or the casting director) can negotiate for as much as you can get for session fees, buyouts, lifts and other kinds of uses like new media and Internet use. Usually advertisers who hire nonunion talent do so because it's a cost savings, not to mention that it doesn't come with the task of tracking where and how often a spot runs. Instead of adding a bunch of small fees together, they'll usually offer talent one flat fee for everything, leaving the actor to decide if it's something they'd be willing to take. This doesn't mean that nonunion actors get ripped off. Agents do their best to get rates comparable with union rates; but not every advertiser out there can pay union rates, and there are plenty of actors who are happy to accept the rates they can pay. Again, as you work, you'll start to decide which path is best for your career.

In some cases, the nonunion agent isn't the entity negotiating the actor's pay. Rates are sometimes agreed upon between clients and casting directors. So if you book a nonunion spot by auditioning at a casting director's office, it doesn't matter which agent you're with, you'll get the same deal as everyone else in town since the casting director negotiated the deal.

Union Industrials

If commercials are the gifts that keep on giving, industrials are the practical, useful gifts from your aunt Eleanor. They're not sexy, but you're glad to get them. Because they're not broadcast, industrials don't have holding fees or other residuals associated with them. You only get your session fee, but the good news is that there are more opportunities to work in industrials than spots. For one, industrials are usually much cheaper to produce, so more companies can afford them. Not every company can spend a million bucks on a commercial, but many can spend $50,000 on a promotional video. Also, producers tend to be incredibly picky when it comes to casting their spots. They want just the right actor for every role, and nothing short of perfection will do. Unless you're exactly what they're looking for, you're not going to get the job. In contrast, there's less emphasis placed on the talent in industrials, and more placed on the message. Even if you're not perfect for the job, you're still in the running if you give a strong audition. Finally, I've been to commercial auditions where I was competing with 100 other actors who looked just like me. Industrials sometimes only audition four or five actors per role. All this means you've got a greater chance of being hired for an industrial than a commercial, and thus a greater chance to make money.

In Chicago, most union industrials fall under the AFTRA Industrial/Educational contract. This agreement spells out different rates for different situations. This gets a little complicated, but according to the union, there are two categories that all industrials fall into: Category I and Category II. The distinction between the two is the intended audience. Videos that are for the company's internal use only fall under Category I. These are usually training videos, or other productions that are not used to sell products, but to inform or otherwise advise the company's workforce about a certain product, policy or issue. Anything that's produced with the intention of showing it to clients, potential customers or anyone who does not work for the company falls into Category II. Those rates are a little higher than Category I. This is because the actor's work is exposed to more viewers, increasing the chance that the actor will become synonymous with that company or product, thereby restricting the actor's future employment options. If you're the spokesperson for Palmolive, you're not going to do a lot of work for other soap brands.

The AFTRA contract also considers what role you're hired for. There are background actors, day players and narrators. If you're a background player, you're an extra and don't have lines. You'll earn $122.50 for an eight-hour day whether the shoot falls into Category I or II. If you're a day player, you've been hired to play a role while not addressing the camera. For example, if you're hired to play a mechanic and your scene consists of a discussion between you and another actor playing the customer, you're both considered day players. Category I day player rate is $471.00 and Category II is $586.00. A narrator's job is to look directly into the camera while delivering the script and provide most of the information the video is trying to get across. Narrator scale is $857.00 and $1015.00 per day for Categories I and II respectively.

There are a lot of special circumstances where these rates can go up, like if you're a stunt performer or if you're a background player with special abilities (like juggling). Check with the AFTRA website for all the variations. SAG also has industrial rates, but we don't see a whole lot of SAG industrials in Chicago.

Recently, agents have been negotiating an additional fee if the video is intended to be posted online. These fees could increase your paycheck as much as 50%. If there's some additional aspect to the project, like a print shoot for banner ads, there will be an extra fee for that use. The details on paying actors for work that will be distributed electronically (online or streamed on wireless devices) are still being worked out by the unions. For now, it's up to the agents to negotiate deals, and it's up to the actors to take them or not.

Nonunion Industrials

If you're a nonunion actor, the pay rates are much more straightforward. You can expect to make more for being a narrator than for being a day player, but that's about where the similarities to the union contract end. Producers and agents work out an actor's fee on a job by job basis. Years ago, my first multi-day industrial paid $250.00 per day. I was hired to play a college kid who needed training on how to use his library's new electronic card catalog (remember, this was before the Internet). All my scenes were with another actor, who played the role of the nice librarian who had all the answers. I was considered a day player. If I were to get that same job today, it would pay closer to $400.00 per day. On camera narrators get somewhere around $750.00 per day for their work, maybe more if they're more experienced, maybe less if the client's budget is tight.

If a nonunion agent is told that the video will wind up online, they'll try to get actors a use fee in addition to the flat payment. They aren't always successful, but when they are, that can add significantly to your pay. These fees might double or triple it, which would mean that you'd actually make more than a union performer if they did the same job.

Whether you're union or not, under certain circumstances you are entitled to extra money in addition to your daily rate. If the industrial requires you to work longer than eight hours, you'll go into overtime and trigger an additional payment based on how long you worked. If you're required to travel to the location, all your expenses will be covered or reimbursed. If you're union, you'll even be given a per diem to cover the cost of eating while you're traveling.

Sometimes however, nonunion producers don't have the budget to pay overtime or travel costs. In these instances, you should be notified beforehand so you can decide whether the job is worth doing. I've heard of nonunion jobs paying a flat rate no matter how long it takes to get the job done. If you're there eight or fifteen hours, you still get that rate. I've also heard of producers from far off locations coming to Chicago for talent, but not wanting to pay for a flight to get them to the shoot. This happened to me. Back in the day I did a narration job in Green Bay, Wisconsin, which is about a five-hour drive from Chicago. At the audition I was told that I'd have to drive up there because there was no budget for a plane ticket. Not wanting to lose the job, I compromised with them and agreed to drive up the day before if they would pay for a hotel the night before the shoot. It worked out fine except that was the last time I worked in Green Bay. For me, it's just too far to go for a job.

Voice Over

Remember my mom's take on voice over work? She thinks it's amazing that people get paid for reading out loud. That's a really simple way to look at this part of the business, but it's not far from the truth. People *do* get paid to read out loud, and if they're very good, sometimes they get paid fantastic amounts.

As a voice talent you can be hired to do a number of different kinds of work. Radio spots, TV spots and longer narration work are the three most common kinds of jobs you're most likely to do in Chicago. Additional opportunities include video games, interactive displays, promos, radio station IDs, phone systems, animated programs, storecasting (those announcements at grocery stores touting the sale of the week), websites, toys and a variety of gadgets that use human voices like the treadmill on which my voice can be heard. You're far less likely to come by these obscure kinds of jobs, and the rates for most of them are negotiated between agents and producers. For that reason, it would be impossible to discuss what you can earn doing these, so I'll stick to the mainstream work.

Union VO

TV spots are a great source of income for voice talent. SAG scale for a TV voice over session is $445.30 per spot. You'll notice that this is less than the scale session fee for on camera work, because you're less likely to be associated with a product (and thus less likely to become overexposed) just by the sound of your voice.

The SAG rates for voice over work follow the same system as on camera work, they're just a little lower. Using our previous example, if you voiced a spot for Target at scale, you'd get $445.30 for the session. If they aired it 50 times under the Class A network rates, you'd be paid $445.30 for the first use, $106.25 for the second, $84.55 for the third through thirteenth and $38.40 for uses 14 and beyond. Remembering that your session includes your first use, your first 13-week total amounts to $2864 for the session and use. Not bad for spending an hour in the studio, but this is only for the first cycle of 13 weeks on network for one spot. If they wanted to continue to air the spot, they'd owe you a holding fee of $445.30, plus whatever usage they'd have to pay. If you did two spots, your earnings would double. And if Target aired the spot on cable or moved it online, they would pay additional fees just like they do when you're on camera. Obviously, the fees can add up to quite a nice chunk of change. Check out the current rates on SAG's website. They're listed right next to the on camera commercial rates in the charts.

Radio spots pay a lot less than TV, but that doesn't mean you can't make good money in that medium. AFTRA scale for a radio session is $262.85 per spot. In contrast to TV, your residuals are paid based on where the spot runs, not on the number of times it runs. For example, if it airs only in Chicago, the producer can buy a wildspot package for $356.95. Just like in TV, your session fee includes the first unit. So your residual payment would be $94.10. If the spot was aired nationally on radio networks, the wildspot fee jumps to $1353.85. The spot can also be run regionally for $817. And if the spot goes online for a year, the fee is $920.00. Again, check the AFTRA site for details. There are no holding fees in radio, but if your spot is renewed after its initial run of six months, you'll be paid another session plus usage. Complicated, I know. That's why it's important to have a good agent to explain this stuff!

When we talk about narration in Chicago, we're usually referring to the industrial kind. Companies are always producing videos that need some kind of voice over narration, and we're happy to have that work. Union actors usually work under the AFTRA contract, and they're paid by the hour instead of by the job. Scale for this kind of session is $385.50 for the first hour and $112.50 for each additional half-hour. That's for Category I, which we know is a project only to be viewed by the company's employees. You get a raise if the public is going to see the video. Category II scale is $429.00 for the first hour and $112.50 for each additional half-hour.

Obviously, the longer the job takes, the more money you can earn. Many narration jobs will take about an hour to complete, but there's no shortage of longer jobs. I've done jobs that have lasted for days. I once narrated a video about paper products that took nearly three days to finish. It's not like I was intentionally screwing up so that I could earn a ton of money, there were just pages and pages of material to get through! I had no idea that paper was such a complicated topic. By the way, if a light bulb just went off over your head, and you're thinking that flubbing your lines is a great way to make more money, I suggest you forget about that idea. Word will get back to your agent, who won't be pleased to hear that their talent was incompetent. Usually agents don't bother working with actors who can't do the job, so each and every time you work, you want glowing reviews to come back from the folks who hired you. Do your best every time or don't bother.

Like their on camera counterparts, there are no residuals on industrial narration jobs, but sometimes agents can negotiate additional fees if the video will be posted online.

Nonunion VO

Nonunion actors don't do too shabby, though they're less likely to get anything other than their session fee. Agents try to negotiate a buyout for TV spots but aren't always successful. Expect to earn around $300.00 to $500.00 per spot, and possibly double that for a buyout that may last a year or more.

When you're nonunion, the more spots you do for a client, usually the less they want to pay you per spot. They figure they're entitled to a discount because they're buying in bulk. It's up to you to decide if this is a good deal for you. Before I joined the unions, I was offered the chance to voice a package of fifteen TV spots for a client. They offered me $275.00 per spot, for a total of $4125.00. I took the deal and was happy to make that much for the two hours of effort the job required. But then I did the math and realized how much money the client saved by hiring a nonunion actor. Between session fees and residuals, they would have easily spent five figures on voice talent had they gone union. I knew that there were companies out there who only hired union talent, and who spent that kind of money all the time. After that job, I started thinking seriously about joining the unions so that I could have the chance to make that much too. Under the union umbrella, there's no discount to producers if they hire you for multiple spots. Again, as you work, you'll form your own opinions about which direction your career should head.

Nonunion radio payments are super straightforward. You get your session and that's it. Expect that payment to be around $200.00 to $400.00 per spot. Buyouts are sometimes offered, but less often than with TV. There are no cycles to worry about in the nonunion world, so your session payment will be the last check you get for that spot.

Along with radio, industrial narration jobs are one area where non-union talent can earn as much, or sometimes more than their union counterparts. Again, agents try to negotiate a session fee and a buyout for a set amount of time, especially if the project is going online. If they're successful, you can earn anywhere from $200.00 to $500.00 for the session, and maybe double that for the buyout.

Print

I love print jobs. Where else can you get paid to sit in front of a camera and smile for a couple hours? Once again, variation is the order of the day. Most print jobs are paid by the hour, and many pay well, but not as well as on camera or VO jobs. Where you might be able to earn about $250.00 for an hour of work doing a radio spot, that same hour spent working a print shoot for a catalog might pay you $175.00. Still, not bad.

Some print jobs pay a lot more than just an hourly rate. If the photos are going to be used for multiple media like online, in brochures and on point-of-purchase displays, you may get an additional usage fee in addition to your hourly rate. This is sort of like the union's residual system except it comes all at once in a lump sum, unlike residual checks, which are spread out over time.

As an example, I once did a job with five other actors for a company that makes barbecue grills. I was booked for an afternoon, about four hours, and the shots were to be used for a bunch of marketing materials. The usage didn't include billboards or magazine ads, but they used them in pretty much every other media outlet for a term of two years. For that I got a flat rate of $1100.00. Pretty good for four hours worth of work.

I've known actors who have earned a lot more from print jobs. When I was just starting out in the business, I had a meeting with an agent who was considering working with me for industrials. When I showed up to meet her, she welcomed me into the office and showed me to her desk, which was right next to another agent's desk. Turns out he ran the agency's print department. During my visit with the industrial agent, the print agent was visited by an actress who wanted to thank him for getting her a job. She was thrilled to have it, but she didn't know exactly how much she was going to make for it. The agent gave her the good news: she cleared about $7000 for the job! I thought "Wow! What would I do with that kind of money?!" She must have read my mind because the first thing she said was, "Great! Now I can pay my taxes." That sort of put the brakes on the celebration, but I was still amazed that you could earn that much just from getting your picture taken.

Ear Prompter

If you're interested in working in industrials, you should seriously consider working with the EAR. While you won't be able to command more money just by being ear prompter proficient, you'll have access to a greater variety of work, and many of those jobs are higher-paying than those that don't require the EAR. That being said, if you have a good command of ear prompter skills, your agent will have an easier time getting you a little more money than she might otherwise.

Virtually all ear prompter jobs will be industrials or trade shows/live events. We'll talk about trade show rates in a moment, and we've already discussed rates for industrials. The EAR is used most often for on camera narration, and AFTRA scale for this work is $857.00 per day for Category I and $1015.00 per day for Category II. Nonunion narrators get around $750.00 per day, maybe a little more. These rates are great, but are starting points. Actors who have been around a while, or who are very good on the EAR can command more.

The other benefit to being a solid ear prompter talent is that you'll be in higher demand than actors who don't use the EAR. Some producers look long and hard for actors who are good with the EAR, and once they find one, they tend to stick with them. Much of my repeat business comes from producers who have used me on the prompter before. Remember, the ear prompter won't come easily to everyone; but if you're able to master this skill, you'll open new doors to future employment.

Trade Shows/Live Events

The trade show business isn't what it used to be. In the late 90's before the dot com bubble burst, I presented at $2000.00 per day. I did several shows a year that were four to six days long. All that money really added up. Today, companies aren't spending anywhere near that much on talent, but you can still earn a nice living doing this kind of work.

Expect a host to earn between $150.00 and $300.00 per day. Crowd gatherers will earn somewhere in the same range. Product specialists earn around $500 per day because they have more training and knowledge. Presenters are paid even more because it's harder to find people who have the unique mix of skills required for the job. Today's day rates for presenters are between $750.00 and $1500.00. As my Dad would say, "Better than a sharp stick in the eye."

There are other kinds of live corporate events that need actors. These aren't trade shows, but more like special events that companies do either for their employees or the public. I once worked at a gathering of retail store managers, and actors were hired to do a play for them. Basically it was a live industrial because the script incorporated issues that the managers would be learning about. Rates for these kinds of events vary widely and can be as little as $200.00 to over $1000.00 per day depending on what you're expected to do.

There's no union that covers trade shows or other live events, so it's up to your agent to negotiate your rate. Occasionally clients will want to videotape your performance for some reason, and you may get additional payment for the video. These videos count as industrials. So if you're union, the AFTRA contract will set the rates, and if you're nonunion, your agent will negotiate any additional money.

TV/Film

Student films, no-budget projects and films on SAG waivers (agreements that defer an actor's payment until the film gets distribution) won't pay much more than $100 per day, if it pays anything. Most of these auditions won't come through your agent since there's no chance they'll make a commission if you book it.

However, your agent *will* be the only way to get paying TV and film work. It will all be SAG or AFTRA work. Both unions have contracts in place for TV and film, and as you can imagine, they have complicated payment structures. So complicated in fact, that for me to give you hard numbers beyond simple day rates would be impossible. I'll explain more on that in a minute.

If you're booked as a principal actor on a TV or film project, you'll be paid for the shoot day (the session) and you'll also get residuals if the project is reused. Book the right project and most of your earnings will come from residuals. Great jobs result in a nice stream of money for years. For work on a film, producers pay residuals if the movie is released on DVD, basic cable, online or on free or pay television. For work on a television show, you'll be paid when the show starts reruns on its original network or is released on DVD, web, pay or free television (syndication) and basic cable. This is part of why actors go after film and TV work. A big movie or top tier TV show can bring in quite a bit of money as it's reused by the producer or distributor. How much? Read on.

This Is The Life

Back in Chapter 1 I told you that I earn a full-time living, but I work part-time hours. I also promised to tell you about a friend of mine. While he gave me permission to tell his story, he preferred that I not use his real name, so I'll call him Ben. About 12 years ago, Ben got his first film role. He landed a spot in the cast of a hugely successful movie. Before that, Ben was an actor from Missouri who worked in St. Louis and Chicago. But after landing that part, he moved to Los Angeles to capitalize on the momentum the appearance brought him. The move was a smart one. Over the years Ben worked on projects as diverse as sitcoms, hour-long dramas, movies of the week and big budget films.

Ben's done a lot of work, but he's not famous. If you saw him on the street you probably wouldn't recognize him, and you definitely wouldn't know his name if you heard it. But he makes a darn good living. In one recent year, Ben earned $170,000. During that year he worked about 36 days. Six weeks! The rest of the time he was off. Residuals make these kinds of numbers possible.

Ben's six weeks' worth of work made him about $30,000 in session fees. The rest of the money came from residuals from his past jobs. Can you believe that? He made about $140,000 in residual income from TV and film appearances done years ago! The unions know that residuals can be critical to an actor's ability to earn a living and because of this, they've put an elaborate system in place to make sure that whenever an actor's face is being seen, the actor's getting paid for it.

Who Gets Paid?

Not extras. Only principal actors whose performance ends up in the final version of the project are entitled to residuals. Even if you spent three weeks on a film set shooting multiple scenes, if your part gets edited out, you won't receive a penny's worth of residuals. Don't worry, you'll still be paid for the time you spent working on the production.

The Numbers

I've been really specific about money. Some of you may have crossed eyes from looking at so many figures. Unfortunately the complexity of the residual system in place for TV and film will make it impossible to do that here. For example, calculating residuals on movies that are streamed online after their initial release is crazy complicated. It depends on who's paying for the content to be online (the consumer or the producer), whether the content is supported by advertising, and whether it's available during, or beyond, a time limit called the "streaming window" among other factors. Going through all of that would be counterproductive. Just know that if you do this work, you'll get what the contracts say you should get.

Let's start with TV. We'll stick with shows shot under the SAG contract for now, although you should know that AFTRA's TV contract is becoming more popular thanks to it's lower rates. Back when the show "ER" was shooting here, many Chicago actors were hired as day performers, meaning they would be paid per day for their services. If you booked a role today on a similar show, you'll get $1051.00 for one day of work if you've never been hired in TV before. Once you have a job or two under your belt, your agent can sometimes negotiate a higher rate, called your "quote". Whether you're booked at scale or at your quote, your session fee includes the episode's initial run, but residuals kick in when it starts to rerun. Assuming it's a network show, the first time the episode reruns in its regular time slot you'd get a payment equal to half of a session fee or $525.50. Beyond that, calculating residuals starts to get tricky. They're based on formulas that consider such variables as the contract in place at the time of the shoot, the time you spent on the production, the production type and the market where the show appears.

Let's say the series goes into syndication, which means it's bought by local network affiliates and aired in non-primetime slots. The formula used to figure an actor's residual for your episode takes into account the number of times you've already been paid. You're given 40% of the scale day rate for the first rerun, 30% for the second, 25% for the third, and on and on until the 12th rerun. At that point you'll earn a payment of 5% of scale every time the show airs thereafter.

It's easy to see that what show your cast in makes all the difference. If you're able to book a role on a series that's really popular, you'll make more in residual payments from that appearance because it's more likely to be rebroadcast more often. Conversely, if you worked on a show that never made it through its first season, you won't make anything beyond your session fee. The same is true for film work. If you show up in a movie that a lot of people want to see, you'll make more than if you're in a film no one cares about. Like TV, no residuals are paid on the film's initial release. Residual payments are due only when the movie is used in other media, like on DVD or pay television.

Film

When a large-budget film comes into town and casts local actors, they're hiring them under SAG's Basic Film Agreement. This contract pays actors like TV shows and commercials do in the sense that actors get session and residual fees. Currently scale for one day of work is $782.00 and $2713.00 for a week. The residual calculations for film are even more complicated than TV because they give weight to actors who were paid more during production. Because of this, I won't be able to give you hard numbers, so I'll just give you the formula instead. Film residuals are usually figured using the production's gross box office receipts after certain deductions are taken. Currently, principal actors share 3.6% of the adjusted gross when the film airs on television. If the movie is released on DVD, the residual is 4.5% of the first million dollars of the adjusted gross and 5.4% on the rest. Remember, principal actors share this number.

But not all films are shot under this particular agreement. SAG has contracts for producers of independent films with much lower rates than the basic agreement. Depending on the budget, an actor could get as little as $100 per day under the ultra-low budget agreement. This agreement allows for residual payments for things like Internet use, but the payments are very low. You can check out the details of this and other low budget contracts at www.sagindie.org.

All residual payments keep coming for as long as the production is generating money for the producer. Even after actors pass away, their heirs continue to get payments on the actor's behalf. Only when the production is mothballed and never used again will the checks stop coming. So you can see that the longer you're working in film and TV, the more money you can make. There are actors who still get checks from sitcoms they worked on in the 1970's!

A Word About Taxes

It's worth noting that your union status will make a difference at income tax time. Nonunion work will pay you in full without holding back any money for taxes. That means the Internal Revenue Service will expect you to pay those taxes when you file your annual return. Union jobs, on the other hand, will nearly always withhold federal, state, and local (if applicable) income taxes. The amount of the withholding will vary, but depends on a multitude of factors such as the information you provide on the IRS form W-4 you'll complete when you do the job, and the state where the job was located. For example, an AFTRA on camera job that shoots in Chicago will have federal and state taxes withheld for Illinois. But one shot in St. Louis will trigger withholding for federal income tax, Missouri income tax, and local St. Louis income tax. That means you'll have to file a return in Missouri as well as Illinois. Ask an accountant how to handle each situation when you file at the end of the tax year. Speaking of working in other markets...

CHAPTER ELEVEN

Working North of the Border

Feel like a nice, relaxing drive? Need some cheese? Hankering for some really fresh Miller Genuine Draft? You can get your fix by driving north about two hours to Wisconsin's most populated city, Milwaukee. But you can do a lot more there than stuff yourself with every kind of cheese you can think of (and some you can't). You can also have an acting career, and a solid, steady one at that.

Milwaukee is a much smaller market than Chicago, but there's a decent-sized production community and a fair amount of work. A lot of Chicago-based actors have decided to join their Milwaukee brethren by working in both markets.

Why would anyone want to work in a city that's two hours away from their home base? One reason is that working in Milwaukee automatically increases your chances of booking a job. It's a numbers thing. If you're multi-listed, you're likely to get more auditions with each agent you add to your list. More auditions lead to more work. Even better, Milwaukee agents have different work available than their Chicago-based colleagues. That means their actors get jobs they wouldn't necessarily get with a Chicago agent. Once in a while there's some cross-over between the two cities, but by and large if you're with an agent from Milwaukee, you're going to be auditioning for stuff that shoots or records there. While there might be fewer jobs available, there are also fewer agents to submit your headshots to, fewer producers to get to know and thus fewer actors vying to get in front of those people. A smaller talent pool is good news for strong actors who can outshine their competition.

Another reason people decide to give Milwaukee a shot is because it's generally more accepting of actors who are new to the business. Because there are fewer actors to choose from, they're much friendlier to newbies. Milwaukee was critical to my career when I was new. One day I was complaining to a teacher about my lack of success in Chicago when he suggested I look into the Milwaukee market. I told him he was crazy because there was plenty of work happening in Chicago. Why would I want to drive two hours to do something I could do here at home? He gently pointed out that although there was plenty of work, I wasn't doing any of it. He also suggested that I would have a hard time getting that work unless my resume reflected my ability to actually do it. In other words, I didn't have any experience. Getting some would make my hunt for an agent, and thus more work, easier.

So I started the process of getting an agent in Milwaukee. Within six months I was listed with all the agents in town, and within a year I was doing a lot of work there. There were times when I had auditions or work in both cities on the same day. There were weeks when I was in Milwaukee more than I was in Chicago. For a couple years, I earned almost half my income up north.

Perhaps even better than the money was the experience I was getting. I proudly put each booking on my resume knowing that the more jobs I listed, the more credibility I'd have with agents in my home town. Each booking was an opportunity to learn something new. I learned to always check your front door for FedEx, even if they usually deliver to your back door (I didn't get a script for a job because the driver left it out front instead of where he usually delivered our packages). I learned to say 'yes' to any job early on because the people you meet might keep you in mind for other work (I was hired over and over by a producer who initially hired me to say one word: "Yes!"). And I learned that if the job calls for you to eat on camera, you don't actually swallow the food (I swear I spat out more cereal on a job than I had actually eaten in my entire life up to that point). I put each new bit of knowledge into my acting tool belt to use later.

But...

Working in Milwaukee is not for everyone. For one, you still have to be good at what you do. Not only are you going to compete against Milwaukee actors, but plenty of Chicago actors will be on the auditions, too. Producers expect high-quality work, and you'll have to be in top form to book these jobs.

The bigger issue is the fact that it's just so far away. When you're listed with a Milwaukee agent, you'll be expected to behave like an actor who lives in the area, meaning you'll have to drive to Milwaukee for auditions. You'll spend four hours on the road for a five-minute appointment. Back when voice over auditions couldn't be done at home, I'd drive up and back to say one line. This kind of time commitment makes it tough to audition in Chicago on days when you have to be up north. You could always cancel on your Milwaukee agent to do something closer to home, but that's a good way to lose that agent. You won't be given any special treatment when it comes to audition time slots. I used to try to get my auditions scheduled in the late morning so I could miss both the morning and afternoon traffic rush, but sometimes I couldn't get those times. And when you land a job, no special arrangements will be made because you're coming from Chicago. You'll have to be up there whenever they need you. I once did a commercial for an appliance store, and they wanted me there at 7:00 AM. They weren't going to pay for a hotel room the night before. I wanted the job, so I got up at four that morning and drove. I was on the set for an hour and made about $300, but I got a credit on my resume.

Here's another thing about Milwaukee: it's almost exclusively a non-union town. A few of the larger ad agencies hire union talent for commercials, but for the most part, members of SAG and AFTRA are shut out of working there. I'm not completely sure why that is, but it's probably got to do with money. The lack of union jobs has made the city a very fertile market for nonunion talent. I found this out firsthand; after making the decision to join the unions, my career in Milwaukee pretty much ended. This actually came at a good time since the constant driving was taking its toll, and I was ready to concentrate on Chicago. While it was tough to lose the relationships I spent years building, it was tougher to lose the money that came with them.

Your Turn

Is working in Milwaukee right for you? Depends on where your priorities lie. If you're willing to do anything to get a foot in the door, pursuing the business in Milwaukee will help you do it. The obstacles to entry are lower, there's plenty of work to be done and there's less competition. Yet those things come at a price for the Chicago actor. It takes large chunks of time out of your day, it causes you to miss auditions in Chicago and it forces you to spend a lot of money on gas. Obviously if you happen to live near the Illinois-Wisconsin border, you'd be crazy not to try working in Milwaukee. You'll have to travel the same distance to get to both cities, so why not give yourself the best chance of succeeding and work both markets?

On the other hand, if your life circumstances aren't conducive to spending the kind of time it will require to build a career there, it's best to focus your efforts in the Windy City. Working in Milwaukee is only a good option for Chicago-based actors who can commit the time and resources to physically get themselves there on a regular basis.

If you do decide to give it a go north of the cheddar curtain (no disrespect intended), there are three talent agencies that dominate the business. I can personally vouch for them because I worked with them all. Check out their websites for submission information, but the process is the same as it is with the agents in Chicago.

Jennifer's Talent Unlimited
740 N Plankinton, Suite 300
Milwaukee, WI 53203
414-277-9440
www.jenniferstalent.com

A full service agency that works in multiple areas of the business, Jennifer's is focused on the Milwaukee market but also has connections nationally.

Aria Talent/Ford Models
807 N Jefferson St # 200
Milwaukee, WI 53202
414-292-3277
www.arlenewilson.com

This is the Milwaukee office of Aria/Ford. They also have an office in Chicago; however, being represented by one does not automatically mean you're with both offices. Formerly known as Arlene Wilson Talent, Aria books work in all areas of the business.

Lori Lins, Ltd.
7611 West Holmes Avenue
Milwaukee, WI 53220
414-282-3500
www.lorilins.com

In business for nearly 30 years, LLL represents talent for all areas of the business.

CHAPTER TWELVE

Working While You're Waiting to Work in Chicago

I want to help get you to a place where you can have an acting career in Chicago. I've spelled out everything you need to know about the process, and I hope you've learned a lot. I'm an eternal optimist and believe that if anyone stays in this business long enough, they'll find some measure of success. Just getting an audition is a minor victory. Getting an agent is a bigger one and getting a job is fantastic. It takes an amazing amount of stars to align for any one actor to land a booking. When this happens to you, consider yourself a successful actor!

However, paired with my optimism is some realism. Your success may not come as soon as you hope. While you're taking classes, chasing down agents and auditioning for work, you'll have bills to pay. If you're going to pursue acting while working in your current career, you've already got enough on your plate. But if you're starting fresh, you may have to think about how to supplement your acting income, at least in the beginning. There are lucky actors who hit the ground running and never look back, and if you're one of those I'm very happy for you. But for the rest of us, it's not a bad idea to think about what else you can do to make ends meet while your career is developing. Many actors have a second or even a third source of income, and I get asked about it a lot when I'm teaching.

In order to have an acting career, you have to be able to audition and work any time Monday through Friday from nine to five. The most important thing about your supplemental income should be its flexibility. You'll need a job that not only makes some cash, but will also allow you to go about the business of being an actor without resulting in the loss of that job. Ideally it should also be something that doesn't bore you to death or crush your natural creativity. I have a friend who temps for extra money, and one of his assignments involved data entry work. His task was to manually enter phone numbers into a database every day for two months. Normally a happy, vibrant and highly creative guy, by the end of it he was depressed, agitated and short-tempered. The mindless repetition of his daily work wore him down. While he was Mr. Data Entry, he was also Mr. I-Can't-Book-an-Acting-Job. He was so unhappy that it affected his performance in front of the camera. He'd tell you that he didn't feel normal again until he did a play. Needless to say, he hasn't done data entry since. You don't want to be him. Pick a job you won't hate.

I've talked to dozens of actors over the years about their second incomes. While none of them were thrilled with the idea of having to prop up their acting career, the ones that were happiest found jobs that fit very well with their own abilities and interests. There are firefighter/actors, cop/actors, massage therapist/actors and on and on. I've got a friend who's always on the same auditions as me. He's very outgoing, always has a smile on his face, and has an easygoing, approachable way with people. In addition to being into acting, he's also a busy real estate agent, which is a great choice for his personality. Being successful in sales requires character traits that he already possesses, so it was just a matter of applying them to the real estate business.

I have another friend who decided to pursue an acting career after she graduated from college with a degree in English. She found a job as a copy editor for a publication. Her office is downtown within walking distance of her agent's office, and her workplace is flexible with her schedule. As long as her work gets finished on time, no one cares when she does it. When she leaves her desk for an hour to audition or work, she stays an extra hour or brings work home to compensate. She gets to combine her love of writing and editing with her love of acting, and best of all, she's happy.

As for me, I've been very fortunate over the years. When I was getting started, I lived with my parents, which allowed me to save a lot of money. Like my buddy the Realtor, I also played the real estate game for a couple of years. It was a job I didn't like, but I used it to meet a very clear objective: to buy my own home. As soon as that happened, the job served its purpose and I quit to focus solely on acting.

The best advice I can give you is to look for a job that could come easily to you. If you grew up using computers, consider an Internet-based job. If you're into exercise, think about becoming a personal trainer or teaching fitness classes. If you love jewelry, find a store that will work with your unusual schedule – there are endless places to look for inspiration. Got any hobbies? Are you passionate about something besides acting? Does someone in the family own a business that might have a place for you? Take a long look at the life you already live, and start there.

So many actors work in restaurants and bars that the idea is cliché, though it's worked out well for lots of them. You won't need any help from me to find a job waiting tables, but if you want other options, you might be stumped. Below are some things that Chicago actors have done while waiting for their career to support them full time.

Driving School Instructor

Yep, you read that right. Someone's got to teach those pesky teenagers how to drive, and since they're in school until the late afternoon, most of the instruction happens on evenings and weekends. Perfect for someone who needs to be available on weekdays! Some schools even let their instructors take the school's vehicles home. Translation: free wheels. If you've got quick reflexes and don't mind the occasional bout of panic, this one could be an actor's perfect second job. Oh, and if you like your motorized vehicles on two wheels instead of four, there are motorcycle schools in town too.

Online Auctions

When I moved out of my parents place and into my first house, I brought everything I owned with me. I didn't prioritize before packing; I just boxed everything up and figured I'd thin it out when I unpacked. Most people do it the other way around, but I'm glad I didn't because right when I moved, I heard about this thing called eBay. Someone told me that people were making more money there than they ever did selling their stuff in garage sales. I looked into it. The short version of this story ends with me being able to make improvements on my new house with the money I got from selling my unwanted stuff on eBay. That was a long time ago when the site really was just for selling old junk. Today, there are many, many people making part- or full-time incomes on eBay. Love hunting for treasure at yard sales? Got a million-dollar record collection that you'd consider parting with? Overburdened with stuff you'll never use? Become an eBay seller and supplement your acting income without ever leaving your house.

E-commerce Website Operator

An actor friend of mine loves art. He also had a lot of free time when his acting career shifted and his income level dipped. So he decided to put his love of art to good use, and he launched a site that sells posters. He and his wife are able to run the whole thing from their home. It makes them some money and it's super flexible so he can still act during the day. You don't have to sell posters. You could sell rubber duckies, handmade purses, or woodworking tools. As long as it brings you some extra cash (and it's legal), who cares what you sell? Got an idea for a website that could be a moneymaker for you? Get on it!

Home-based Businesses

There are plenty of companies out there that allow you to sell their products from your home. Everything from skin care to jewelry to housewares can be bought at a discount from the manufacturer and sold by you. You don't work for the companies. Instead you act as an independent distributor so you set your own schedule. It can be tricky to make these kinds of businesses profitable, but if you're a self-starter and relentless about pursuing success, they can be perfect for actors. Search online for them, or start with these: Lia Sophia, Tupperware, Pampered Chef, Mary Kay Cosmetics, Arbonne International or Amway.

Advertising Guy/Girl

Sometimes actors and voice talent come out of the advertising industry. It's either because as ad agency people they saw so many bad auditions that they thought they could do a better job, or because they were closet actors when they got their ad job in the first place. But there's nothing that says you can't start as an actor and wind up getting hired at an agency. If you studied marketing, art or writing in college, you may be able to work as an account rep, art director or copywriter. These kinds of jobs may not provide the level of flexibility you're looking for, but they'd put you in the position of learning an awful lot about how actors are cast in commercials. There are a couple actors in town who have worked at agencies while pursuing an acting career. They all said the same thing: you have to earn the right to be able to leave the office during the day for auditions by being very good at what you do.

Houses Of Worship

If you happen to be an active member at a church, temple or other place of worship, you might look there to see what's available. A friend of mine heard that his church was looking for a bookstore manager, and he wound up getting the job. His longest day is on Sunday, which never conflicts with his acting, and he's able to get other days off during the week. It was a good match for him because it provided money and flexibility, and it lined up with his core values.

Health Clubs/Gyms

If you're a regular at your gym, you might as well be getting paid for it. Members usually make good employees because they're already invested in the club, and management knows this. There are a couple ways to stay fit and make a little extra on the side. All fitness centers need someone to work the front desk or do other jobs at all hours of the day. Check with yours to see if there's an opening. Employees usually get steep membership discounts, too. If you love your yoga, Pilates or spinning class, think about teaching one. Most classes are scheduled in the early mornings or in the evenings. Check into the requirements to become an instructor. Or, you could go for your personal training certification. Ask your gym which one they require their trainers to achieve. All of these options allow you to keep time open for your acting and put extra money in your pocket.

Temp/Office Work

Not everyone has horrible experiences with temping like my buddy Mr. Data Entry. In fact, lots of people find permanent jobs through temping. Temp agencies allow you to pick the days you want to work, along with the jobs you want to work. Julia Merchant, a VO artist in Chicago, has had good luck with temping. She worked at a variety of offices before finding one with which she clicked. They got to know her and offered her a full-time position. Since she was open about her acting, they knew she needed flexible scheduling, and because she was a good employee, they agreed to work with her. Julia says, "I feel lucky that I found a boss who gets it. He's been on the board of a couple of theater companies, and he's sympathetic to the needs of actors." This is a great situation and one that every actor hopes to fall into.

You can make it happen with a little homework. Look up board members of big time theater companies in town. A little digging online can tell you what they do for a living. Many of these folks will own businesses. You can start your job search at these companies, where you'll have a better chance of working for someone who understands that actors sometimes have to manage their time differently than other employees.

Standardized Patient Work

Part of a med student's education has always been working with patients in a clinical setting, but most medical schools are augmenting the students' training with standardized patient programs. Actors are hired to portray patients and interact directly with med students in simulated doctor visits. This kind of work requires actors to be familiar with a patient profile and to be able to answer questions related to the illness or symptoms they "have." Basically, you're hired to play a sick person who's visiting their doctor for help. These jobs require a little improvisation within the framework of the background information you're given. The goal of these programs is to train med students to respond to patients' needs in a professional and compassionate way. In addition to being fairly flexible, this is important work. You'll be helping teach tomorrow's physicians, which is good for all of us, and you'll be sharpening your acting skills while you do it. The medical schools at Loyola University, Northwestern University, the University of Chicago, Midwestern University and the University of Illinois at Chicago all have these programs. Check their websites for details about applying.

Intern At An Agent's Office/Casting Office

I hesitate to suggest this since I'm trying to help you find jobs that make money and don't get in the way of your acting. Internships don't pay, but boy are they an education. A lot of actors intern with an agent or casting director. If you're interested in learning about the business from a side you'll never see as an actor, you couldn't do better than an internship with these folks. Not all offices have openings, so you might have to send a few emails to see who does. Sometimes interns wind up getting hired, which shouldn't be your focus since you're trying to be an actor, but you may find the casting process fascinating. Many actors do, and some switch their focus. Lots of agents and casting directors start out as actors. There won't be any money in an internship, but there may be a new career in it for you. If the idea intrigues you, don't hesitate to check it out.

Be Upfront

If you talk to actors about their second jobs, you're bound to hear some interesting stories. One actress, when she was interviewing for her first job out of college, told her prospective employer that she was first and foremost an actress. She made it clear that she didn't want any responsibility, to have a set schedule, or be in a position where she would need to care about her work. In other words, she needed the job, but didn't want to be held accountable for anything. To my shock, she went on to say that they hired her as a receptionist! I think that's the actor's pipe dream: to find an employer who will pay you for the least amount of commitment that you can muster. She was lucky. I don't recommend that you go around saying that you won't care about a job that you're hoping to get.

That does bring me to a point that many actors made about their second jobs. Even though this actress said all the things you shouldn't say at an interview, at least she told them that she was going to be pursuing another line of work. No matter where your second job is, it's important to be honest about everything before you accept the position. All of the actors I talked with said that telling their bosses about their acting *before* they started the job was critical to keeping the peace once they had the job. Employers who didn't know that their new hires would be asking for a lot of time off were much less likely to be flexible.

Another point that came up a lot was the issue of balance. One voice talent who also works in an office said she puts a lot of effort into making each job feel as though it's her top priority. "I try to treat both jobs with the same amount of respect. Both have expectations that are important to fulfill, and I work hard at balancing them. If I'm going on a business trip, I book out with my agent and make sure they know when I'm back. I've laid a lot of groundwork at my office by stepping up and making myself indispensable there. That's made it easier for my bosses to give me the flexibility I need to come and go during the day."

Another actor put it this way, "I don't want to sound like a jerk, but I'm given some freedom at work because I'm really good at my job. I hustle my tail off to produce at the highest level every single day. If I didn't,

I'd have a target on my back. There are people there who don't like that I go after my acting career as hard as I work at my desk. And I hate it when someone asks if I'm acting full time. Am I on a sitcom? No. But I'm out there every day auditioning and taking the opportunities that come my way. So yeah, I'm a full-time actor."

It's very possible to have another job and make it work with your acting career. The keys are to be open with your superiors, and treat both those in the acting world and those in your other world as if they're too important to lose.

Seasonal Patterns

By now you know that the business of acting is unpredictable. Certain times of the year will be very busy and others quiet. It's impossible to tell when your business will soar or dip, but over the years I've noticed certain patterns. I have no hard numbers to back any of this up, but if you do this long enough, you begin to notice things. For example, you can almost certainly count on the business slowing down around the holidays. From Thanksgiving to New Year's Day, people are thinking about anything but work, and by "people" I mean ad agencies and producers. As a result, there's usually a noticeable drop in the stuff that keeps actors busy: auditions and bookings. For this reason, a lot of actors work retail during the holidays.

Summertime can also be quieter than the rest of the year, because a lot of people take vacations during that time. Many ad agencies have summer hours with Friday afternoons off. In June, July and August productivity is down, meaning actors have more free time. Some use it to do more theater, maybe at regional theaters in other parts of the Midwest.

During the rest of the year, work is usually pretty steady. There's enough happening to keep everyone active both on the union and non-union side. I did notice something weird, but pretty consistent, when I was nonunion. The weeks before and after a three-day weekend seemed to be slow. I could almost count on having nothing going on for two weeks around Memorial Day, Labor Day and other holiday weekends. Since I went union, however, that changed, so I can't say if that trend continues today.

Keep in mind that these are very general observations from years of watching the business ebb and flow, and by no means are they hard fact. I've had years where I was slammed with work around the holidays. In fact, I once turned down a job that was scheduled to shoot on Christmas Eve. I've also had very slow starts to the year, only to be surprised by a very active summer season. You really can never tell what business is going to be like at any given moment.

CHAPTER THIRTEEN

Off You Go

C onsider yourself armed with the information you'll need to navigate this crazy business in this most sensible of towns. I hope you feel more prepared than you did before reading this book.

I want to leave you with one last story. My first voice over teacher said a lot of things that I still remember to this day, but the most important went something like this, "Remember that the longer you stay in this business, the more of a veteran you'll be, even if you hardly ever work." It was his way of telling me that persistence will be the key to my career.

Do you have any idea how many people want to be actors? Tons. Just ask any agent. Their mailboxes are packed with new faces every day, people who want their shot at getting paid to do what they love. Now consider this: do you have any idea how many of those people start the process only to abandon it shortly thereafter? Again, I'd say tons. Breaking into this business almost never comes easily to anyone. Once a door has opened, making the jump from newbie to working professional is even harder. Competition is friendly, but heated. For any given audition, there's no shortage of actors who really need the job, so everyone does their absolute best every time they're given the chance. You must perform up to that level, or you'll always be watching the Lost Audition Channel on cable. You know, the one where you see who booked all the jobs you auditioned for.

I don't know if they still do this, but medical schools used to drive a point home to their new students by gathering them together in an auditorium on their first day. The students are told to look to their left, then to their right. Then they're told that one of those people will not be there on graduation day, and thus not become doctors. The day you send your first headshot to an agent is the same day dozens of other people do the same thing. Many of them won't even follow up, let alone be called in for an interview. Those that do land representation will audition a few times, then might give up when they don't book anything. Or they'll lose faith when their agent doesn't call them for a while and they'll drop out of the business.

So where will you be? Still in the trenches, I hope. The longer you hang in there, the more familiar your name will become with those who can help you. At some point a door will open, and you'll be there to walk through it while many of your peers who started with you will have fallen by the wayside. Even if you haven't booked a single thing, you're a veteran of the business by default.

If you're persistent and professional, you'll begin to work. As you do, don't be discouraged by dry spells. Everyone has them, even me. Remember, in the Dark Ages when I had a pager and if I hadn't heard from anyone in a while I'd page myself to make sure the stupid thing was still working? Today, I still sometimes look at my phone and wonder, "Is it me, or is everyone slow?" Expect that you'll have long stretches of time between auditions and jobs. It's part of being an actor.

I'm a full time actor only because I was, and still am, persistent. I had plenty of reasons to quit, but I want to be here too much. Sometimes it comes down to just that - do you want to be an actor? If so, then do it. People will tell you it's not possible. They mean well, but they're wrong because obviously it's very doable. Don't take their negativity in. Just keep going. Stay in the game. Keep auditioning, networking, training and you'll book work. Before you know it, you'll be in the business for as long as you can remember and you'll be writing books to help others accomplish the same thing.

Instead of wishing you luck, tradition says I'm supposed to wish you broken limbs. I always thought that was silly, so good luck to you! May you always get what you want out of this business.

Acknowledgements

Books are hard to write. Don't ever let anyone tell you otherwise. Since I'm an actor and not a writer, I looked for a life raft or two. Or fifty. This book only became a reality because of the generosity of others, and I can't thank them enough. Brett Thompson was a fantastic research assistant, production coordinator and amateur lawyer. Kristi Wenz and Staci Falk kept the text clear, while Laura Shatkus, Joanna Krupa, Vanessa Dewing and Becca Coren Lasser gave me a lot to think about. Content was cleared up by Rachel Patterson, Duane Sharpe, Jerris Breslin, Sean Bradley and Kathleen Hennon. Other important contributions were made by Freddie Sulit, Richard Schoen, Christian Heep, Chris Garrett, Julia Merchant, Sharon Wottrich, Saskia Bolore, Brian King, Holmes Osborn, Samantha Glistein and Stephon Fuller. Without Ray Van Steen, Anne Jaques and Kurt Naebig, my acting career wouldn't be what it is today and this book wouldn't exist. I thank Sam Samuelson for risking his good name on a first-time author's work. And I thank my wife, Patricia, for risking her happiness by marrying me. This project wouldn't have been finished without her bottomless cup of love and encouragement.

About the Author

CHRIS AGOS began his acting career in 1995. Known for his efficiency and professionalism on the job, producers have cast him in every kind of work the Chicago market has to offer. He continues to audition, work and teach other actors how to navigate the choppy waters of the acting world every day. He lives in Evanston, Illinois with his wife and twin sons.